Welsh-born Mark Dodd grew up in Queensland and Victoria. After dropping out of art school he tried his hand at a variety of jobs before a trek through the top end led him to Broome and to pearl diving. After leaving Broome, Mark worked as a journalist – based for more than a decade in East Africa, Southeast Asia and notably in East Timor during its violent transition to independence. He currently works for *The Australian*, and lives in Canberra, Australia.

The LAST PEARLING LUGGER

The LAST PEARLING LUGGER

A pearl diver's story

MARK DODD

Pan Macmillan Australia

First published 2011 in Macmillan by Pan Macmillan Australia Pty Limited
1 Market Street, Sydney

Copyright © Mark Dodd 2011

The moral right of the author has been asserted.

All rights reserved. No part of this book may be reproduced or transmitted by any person or entity (including Google, Amazon or similar organisations), in any form or by any means, electronic or mechanical, including photocopying, recording, scanning or by any information storage and retrieval system, without prior permission in writing from the publisher.

National Library of Australia
Cataloguing-in-Publication data:

Dodd, Mark.

Last pearling lugger / Mark Dodd.

ISBN: 9781742610498 (pbk.)

Dodd, Mark.
Pearl divers – Western Australia – Broome – Biography.
Pearl industry and trade – Western Australia – Broome – History.

639.412099414

Typeset in 12.5/16.5 pt Sabon by Midland Typesetters Australia
Printed by McPherson's Printing Group in Australia

Papers used by Pan Macmillan Australia Pty Ltd are natural, recyclable products made from wood grown in sustainable forests. The manufacturing processes conform to the environmental regulations of the country of origin.

This book is dedicated to my family, my late mother, Dad, Simon and Christina, Ying and Yang, Sian, George and Tom. It's been a long time coming.

Contents

A note about measures	xi
Preface: The brass corselet	1
1. The Kimberley	5
2. Broome	19
3. Lugger buggers	31
4. The stuffer patches	47
5. The Japanese	63
6. The twelve-tonne haul	77
7. The cashed-up Colonel	91
8. Diving in	101
9. The Roey	119
10. At sea on the B-3	129
11. Ramah and friends	143
12. The season from hell	155
13. Introducing 'Dad'	173
14. Back to the *DMcD*	185
15. Dabbling in new waters	193
16. Falling apart	203
17. The end of an era	215
Epilogue: Turning for port	225
Notes on the text	237
Acknowledgements	239

A note about measures

This book uses metric and imperial measures because both were used interchangeably in the pearling industry in the late seventies and early eighties.

10 feet = 3.048 metres
10 metres = 32 feet, 9.75 inches
1 fathom = 6 feet
1 fathom = 1.8288 metres
1 nautical mile = 1.852 kilometres

PREFACE:

The brass corselet

A gentle dip in the northwest shoulder of the Australian continent marks Eighty Mile Beach at the western extremity of the Great Sandy Desert.

It is a stretch of coastline that I know well. For five years I worked on pearling luggers and sailed up and down the Eighty Mile on a variety of boats, in all weather conditions, at every time of day and night. I can still name every bay, cape, promontory and creek for 100 kilometres or more south of Broome.

At first light, I'd gaze at the friendly, fuzzy olive outline of the beach as I took my ritual morning piss off the stern of the *DMcD*, one arm braced for support against the creaking boom on the mizzen mast. (Needless to say, there were no heads on the old luggers.) Daylight revealed the Eighty Mile for what it was: save for the odd cattle station, a bleak and desolate stretch of rolling sandhills amid pockets of waterless pindan scrub.

During the dry, it glowed red as bushfires blazed along its shore; but on days when everything was obscured by a clammy grey swirling mist and the only sound was the slapping of a gentle, oily swell against the side of the boat, then the Eighty Mile took the form of a green spidery, phosphorescent line on the radarscope.

In time its bluffs and promontories became well-worn references on our charts, aiming points for radar buoys marking the location of patches of wild pearl shell, or dumps for shell that we had harvested and cleaned in readiness for pearl culture.

There had been many luggers here before us. The seabed was one vast watery graveyard. Cyclones had taken a heavy toll on the early pearling fleets. One ferocious storm in 1887 sent thirteen boats to the bottom with the loss of 140 lives. Before the first primitive engines were fitted onto luggers in 1910, if you got caught in a blow while working the Eighty Mile, there was almost no chance of escaping alive.

Even steamers were at risk. While working the southern end of the Beach we would watch out for the wreck of the old state ship *Koombana*, lost with all hands in 1912. Lightly ballasted and bound for Broome, she was last seen near Port Hedland, her huge prop churning through the sea. She ran headlong into a cyclone and disappeared, presumably sunk to the bottom. An empty lifeboat and her stateroom door were the only traces of her ever found.

THE LAST PEARLING LUGGER

Among the 138 crew and passengers who had vanished was a Melbourne pearl buyer by the name of Abraham Davis, owner of a fabled gem pearl known as the Roseate Pearl. It was said to be pink, perfectly round, and worth £20,000. The story goes that it was also cursed, and that several men associated with it died violent deaths.

Such superstitions are rife in the pearling business, and not surprising given the risks invariably taken to uncover natural pearls, especially back in the traditional era of hard-hat diving when men garbed in heavy metal helmets and canvas body suits combed the sea bottom off Broome, a thin air line tended by a deckhand their only connection to safety.

I became a pearl diver in the late seventies, when modern diving methods had only recently replaced the hard-hat method. On many a long, bone-numbingly cold dive, as the lugger dragged me across some barren outcrop of sea bottom in search of pearl shell, I would kill time fantasising about the scores of pearling vessels whose final resting place lay somewhere below my trajectory.

One day in 1982, we were drifting in relatively shallow water in the Lacepede Channel when I floated over the rotting remains of an old boat.

The visibility that morning was almost perfect. Fifteen metres or so below me, illuminated by a long shaft of blonde light, I could make out the vague outline of what I took to be a lugger. A few ribs, a cast-iron engine block, and then something else caught my eye: a perfect circle of marine growth. Punching my gloved fist into the growth I was able to insert my arm through what appeared to be a heavy metal ring. Excitement gripped me as I realised that the sea was giving up one of her secrets. As the lugger moved on and tension took up on my work line, the metal remains came free in a cloud of marine debris.

Back on deck I scrubbed my find with a wire brush. What was revealed was a brass corselet, the metal body armour that in a traditional pearl diver's rig sits over the shoulders, directly below the copper helmet or hard-hat. This one bore the famous toolmaker's stamp 'Heinke of London', dated 1894. Something had bent the corselet almost in half. What huge force was responsible, I could only speculate.

During ensuing dives over the years my crewmates and I often found relics of the past, bits of copper cladding, old anchors, a length of encrusted chain, an occasional engine block covered in coral, or a rotting keel distinguished only by the marine growth feeding off it. But to their disappointment, even the most experienced divers I know never matched my find. There was an element of serendipity involved, as there always is in pearl fishing.

Today the brass corselet takes pride of place atop an old Cambodian timber dresser in my lounge room. It's my connection with the romance of the men (and occasionally the women) who worked the traditional pearling luggers out of Broome. It reminds me that, for a few brief years, I was one of their number. It also reminds me that during those years the pearling industry changed irrevocably, along with Broome itself. I was a witness to those changes.

CHAPTER 1

The Kimberley

My mate Al Burton and I rolled into Broome late one afternoon in 1978, drawn there by other travellers' tales of fabled Cable Beach. After months on the road, we were in the mood for some serious R and R. Hard travel had reduced the charms of living off the land – my gums were raw and bleeding from our limited diet. I needed a dentist. I wanted a swim and a cold beer, not necessarily in that order.

We had set out from Melbourne in Al's old Land Rover to follow the original Ghan train line from Port Augusta up to Alice Springs. There we had turned left, veering northwest along the Tanami Track to Halls Creek and into the Kimberley, the vast wilderness at the far northern end of Western Australia.

For more than three months we had explored the Kimberley's densely forested bluffs, rocky gorges and rich savanna. We had slept in our swags in caves or on the grasslands where more than a hundred years ago Europeans had first started running cattle. Station owners or managers for the most part welcomed us, letting us camp and fish on their properties in return for shooting vermin, particularly the feral donkeys which gathered in mobs around water holes, depriving cattle of a drink.

Al, a builder, had been born on Bow River Station, a huge spread on a tributary of the Ord River which was once part of the Durack family's pastoral empire but had since been returned to the local Aboriginal people. Our trip was his idea. He wanted to hunt, fish and explore the wild country that he remembered from his earliest childhood. It sounded good to me.

I had had a peripatetic upbringing, born in Wales, then raised in Herefordshire before my family emigrated to Australia when I was nine. My father was a livestock liaison agent for J.C. Hutton's, ham and bacon manufacturers. We settled on the outskirts of Brisbane in Moggill, then a predominantly rural area. Our nearest neighbour, Mrs Waldie, was a dairy farmer. In a uniform of bib-and-brace overalls and broad brim straw hat, she rode her battered red Massey-Ferguson tractor, faithful cattle dog never far behind her.

My mum was a free spirit and would often set up her easel in the nearby paddock, rendering an impression of the bush landscape around our old Queenslander home, the handsome peak of Mt Flinders in the distance. When I was not helping Dad with fencing or myriad

THE LAST PEARLING LUGGER

other chores around the property I would steal off with my schoolmates for extended fishing outings along the big brown Brisbane River. It was a working river with coal barges coming down from the nearby Bremer and gravel barges from local quarries. I learnt to ride at an early age, as did Simon and Sian, my younger brother and sister. My horse, a mare called Emma Peel, was half-thoroughbred and half-camp drafter, bred in the flat country around Dalby where she had never heard a motorbike. The first time I rode to pony club, an unmuffled Harley drove by and she smartly ejected me from the saddle. In fact I spent quite a lot of time getting tossed off the saddle, including getting my foot caught in a stirrup during an impromptu buck jumping exhibition by my previous mount, a semi-feral pony called Ali who happily dragged me across the length of the front paddock.

When Dad was promoted to head office the family moved to Melbourne. Though we settled in the suburbs, I never lost the taste for life outside the big cities.

By the time Al and I became friends I was an art school drop-out, full of seventies idealism and influenced by my obsessive reading of the English journalist and author George Orwell. It was not Orwell's radical politics that inspired me so much as his determination to look reality square in the eye and to write about it just as bluntly. Adventurous, determined to discover what lay beyond the middle-class circumstances in which he was born, he became an imperial police officer in Burma, stationed there for several years before dengue fever did his health in. Then it was back home where, in Jack London style, he lived and worked among the poor of the East End and Paris, and later the North of England, writing about what he saw.

To my parents' despair, I turned my hand to a series of blue-collar jobs, hoping to do an Orwell and transform myself into a journalist in the process. I tried out for a day as a garbo and immediately discovered just how fit you needed to be. First morning on the job, my workmates were all A-grade footy players from the local club at Ringwood. They used the early morning round for training. After three hours jogging non-stop through the back roads of Mitcham I could barely heave a bin into the truck. Embarrassing to remember the trails of spilt garbage I left scattered across neat front lawns in Melbourne's leafy outer east.

So, I was a failed garbo but I fared better at subsequent jobs: labouring, gardening, driving, factory work and then, finally, something interesting – powder monkey on the construction of the Sugarloaf Dam in the Yarra Ranges east of Melbourne.

My boss was a bloke called Jet Jackson. He had all his fingers, despite his name, and unlike many powder monkeys. The work involved preparing two-tonne mixes of ammonium nitrate and diesel, which were combined in a cement mixing truck. Air track drillers were used to perforate the quarry face with dozens of holes. Into the holes we lowered triple sticks of AN-60 dynamite attached to red detonating cord. Then the ammonium nitrate mixture was poured into the shot holes. Colour-coded detonators were fixed to the cord and wired into a wonderfully named instrument called a Beethoven Exploder, and – preferably – ignited from the safety of a bulldozer bucket.

THE LAST PEARLING LUGGER

I earnt enough to fix up my four-wheel drive for a trip north to Cape York. Returning flat broke several months later, I took a job as a gardener on a flower farm in the Dandenong Ranges. Soon I graduated to heavy salvage, working for a wrecking company which specialised in buying up old factories and houses in inner Melbourne and renovating them for sale with prime period pieces salvaged from demolition. One job in St Kilda involved wrecking an old Commonwealth Bank. It was the last assignment of the day, and the light was beginning to fade when I pulled up in the tip truck with my heavily tattooed assistant, who looked like he had just been released from Pentridge's H Division. By the time we had fired up the gas and started cutting through the bank's iron bars quite a crowd had gathered opposite, watching what they thought was a bank heist. The police arrived, and we explained that this branch of the Commonwealth had temporarily relocated. They looked doubtful.

Salvage involved using a bobcat, a jemmy bar and a sledgehammer. I went home absolutely knackered, my mouth and hair and eyes full of concrete dust. As backbreaking and mind-numbing as manual work often was, it had its rewards. Meeting all sorts of people – real people, as I thought of it – was one. Competence was another. It was satisfying to master a potentially dangerous process, whether learning how to control a three-tonne truck or pull a beautiful old fireplace from a wonky brick wall in the middle of a half-demolished building. Later in Broome, where the work was physically harder than anything that I had ever experienced, there was a sort of grim pleasure in the painstaking task of efficiently cleaning and packing pearl shell for export.

In preparation for our trip, I sold my own off-roader after stripping the old clunker of any useful bits, including one very serviceable set of heavy-duty rear springs to manage the new expedition load. Flush with the proceeds of this sale, I bought a little fibreglass punt and a two-stroke outboard which we would use to explore the Kimberley rivers and Lake Argyle. These went into a ruggedised box trailer towed by Al's Land Rover, a short-wheel-base, series two, 1959 model that was fitted with a powerful three-litre Rover motor lifted out of a saloon.

Most importantly we packed our rifles, Al's a scoped .308 repeater, mine a customised Springfield Mauser action 30/06. (It was an irony of the pacifist sixties that many teenage boys like me learnt to handle a gun as members of school cadet corps.) Before we left Melbourne, I took advantage of a hand-loader rigged in a friend's backyard gun shed to fashion some thumping power loads, in case we ran into a scrub bull or something higher on the food chain that might take a dislike to us.

When we reached Alice Springs I made a further addition to our armoury, a single-shot 12-gauge shotgun for small game. In the gun shop there were no questions asked. The owner just took my money, handed over the hardware and wished me 'good hunting in the Todd River'. I realised with a shock of disbelief that this was a reference to the Aboriginal people camped on the local riverbed, many of them in a terrible condition from grog. It was my first experience of the flagrantly racist jocularity that is part of life in the north.

So far the trip had been relatively easy going. On our way up, we had camped in the South Australian desert, sometimes in crumbling stone cottages which provided good shelter at night, at least until the bone-freezing chill set in. In Alice, we had stayed a few days with an old friend of mine from art school, Norm House, who was living there with his girlfriend, Karen. It was August, and we had about three months of decent travelling conditions before the Wet set in. We were keen to get going, to give ourselves plenty of time in the Kimberley before the season of wash-outs and rising rivers began.

Loading up the Land Rover with supplies, we set off north up the Stuart Highway, then onto the Tanami Track and up to the old mining town of Halls Creek, in the east Kimberley. This leg, 800 kilometres of four-wheel driving over a historic sand track that miners and geologists had followed ever since gold was first discovered in this remote desert region, was a chastening experience which taught us not to underestimate the hazards ahead. We were carrying only one spare tyre, which we used on the first day. When a second tyre went, staked by a sapling, Al and I were not particularly fazed. We knew we had the skills to patch the slashed inner tube and get it back into the tyre, so that we could limp on to Rabbit Flat and get a proper replacement there. What we didn't account for was the spectacular sandstorm which hit us half-way through the complicated repair job. We had just enough time to finish and stash away our tools, pull a tarp over the Land Rover's engine and radiator, and hunker down inside the car before a wall of brown sand swept over us. For fifteen minutes, willy-willies buffeted the vehicle, battering the exterior like a sand-blast. Just as suddenly as it came, the storm was gone.

We had been lucky: the four-wheel drive came through unscathed. We drove on gingerly. Rabbit Flat, which turned out to be an isolated roadhouse and nothing more, underlined the surrealism of our recent experience. We met a Dutch traveller there who was recently arrived from Yuendumu, an Aboriginal community further south. The only English that he owned had been picked up from his indigenous hosts, and the results were gibberish: the local creole spoken with a heavy Dutch accent. Not that it stopped him talking.

* * *

WHEN I drove from Kununurra to Broome a few years ago to complete the research for this book, I was amazed by how much had changed since Al and I ventured into the Kimberley together. The Great Northern Highway which runs along the southern edge of the Kimberley is now double-lane blacktop all the way from Port Hedland to Darwin. During the dry winter months, it is packed with fleets of tourists, Australian and international, dragging caravans behind their four-wheel drives, camping in tourist parks, and dining at the occasional fast food restaurants that have sprung up along the route.

Thirty years ago, road travel in the Kimberley was a much more hazardous proposition. Not only was more of the road network unsealed, there was also much less traffic on it. In those days before mobile phones, to break down or run out of fuel would mean a lonely wait by the side of the track, hoping that a cattle transport or mining company vehicle would pass.

THE LAST PEARLING LUGGER

Al and I headed north from Halls Creek up to the Bow River, where we spent a week or so fishing. Then we struck off onto the Gibb River Road, an old cattle track which winds for more than 600 kilometres through the red-brown sandstone ranges of the northwest between Derby, the area's major port, and the outskirts of Kununurra. It was unsealed, sharply rocky in parts of the eastern side, and pitted with corrugations and old wash-outs from previous wet seasons. Stopping at the Mowanjum Aboriginal community just out of Derby, we sought and received permission from tribal elders to visit their traditional land at Walcott Inlet, which is famous for its fishing.

To reach this remote spot, we had to double back, driving 300 kilometres up the Gibb River Road to Mt Elizabeth Station. From there, it was a vicious bush bash over more than 200 kilometres on a rough track pioneered by the legendary drover and pastoralist Frank Lacy, who had settled Mt Elizabeth in 1945. We broke the journey, camping for a couple of days a few hundred metres from the Lacy homestead. At night, Frank, who was then in his eighties, would come out to our campfire, and over his preferred tipple, a pannikin of rum, enthral us with yarns about his days droving in the Kimberley. He had helped sink bores in the Tanami during the Granites gold rush before he became a cattleman. He told us how he had sometimes spotted Japanese Zero fighters flying unescorted while he drove stock down this track during the war. The Jap planes were searching for the 'secret' bomber base at Truscott, near Kalumburu mission. The impact of aviation on this last frontier must have been amazing. Frank showed me an old pearl shell carved by local Aboriginals, depicting the first bi-plane to fly into the region. It had been given to him on a visit to Derby in the 1920s.

Frank had married an Aboriginal woman, Theresa, which was unusual for the time. In Western Australia, the marriage of indigenous women was for many years controlled by law. Intending husbands needed permission from the authorities, and obtaining it could be a difficult process. Often they just cohabited with Aboriginal women, though this was technically illegal too. There was no doubt that the indigenous people of the Kimberley had copped a tough time from the authorities before racial discrimination was finally outlawed in the 1970s. Frank talked at length about the 1915 Mistake Creek massacre of local Aboriginals in the East Kimberley, payback by 'special constables' for cattle spearing. He told the story in such terrible detail that we could not help but wonder if he or someone close to him had been a witness to it.

It was a major effort to get into Walcott. There was little left to see of the former Munja mission and leprosarium which had once stood there, but we did find an ideal campsite next to a tidal reach thick with barramundi. The river was full of saltwater crocodiles, so we seldom strayed far without our rifles. We camped far back from the water, and as a further precaution kept our fire burning at night while we slept.

Back on the Gibb River Road, we decided to take a detour up the Kalumburu Road to the Mitchell Falls, a stunning sequence of waterfalls which descended through a series of blue pools on the Mitchell River. The area was remote, but accessible. Travelling was slow, and you had to be patient. It had taken us two days to drive out from Walcott Inlet along a very rough track, in some places nothing more than jagged rocky outcrops.

En route to Kalumburu we called into Drysdale River Station for fuel, and ended up making an extended stay. After a few very welcome cold beers, the station manager, Rex Dickson, asked for help to get a 'killer', a barren cow that is killed for meat for the cool store.

We rode out in Rex's four-wheel drive. He selected a beast and stopped the vehicle so I could get a head shot. A chest shot would have been easy but the station manager liked eating brisket and requested 'one in the brain'. The rifle – a .243 calibre – belonged to Rex and I was unfamiliar with it. Firing open sights without a scope I overcompensated the distance – the cow was walking – and severely injured her in the lower jaw.

Bellowing with pain, she took off at a gallop. We gave chase. Cursing my botched marksmanship, Rex seized the rifle and dispatched the beast with one shot. I had learnt a valuable lesson the embarrassing way. Never again would I volunteer to kill an animal using an unfamiliar weapon.

The cow got me back. After weeks in the bush on a hard tack diet, I found that my health was starting to suffer. We had no fridge, and, save for a dwindling quantity of spuds and onions, our supply of fresh vegetables would soon be exhausted. An unvaried diet of potatoes, onions and freshwater fish or station meat caused my gums to bleed. At a barbecue at Drysdale River Station, I realised that I could barely chew, my teeth and gums were so sensitive.

Al and I helped Rex with some fencing and some welding repairs on his trailer. In return, before we left he showed us some spectacular cave art lying in the bush a short distance away from the main Kalumburu track. It featured Wandjinas (rain gods), eerie white figures shrouded in cloaks of rain, their heads surrounded by circles of lightning and cloud, the eyes large and round, the mouths and chests shrouded in fog. The rain god was the Creator, building the first man out of mud or clay, then the first woman, then all the animals of the Earth. The people that he made recorded their stories in caves or other sacred sites that were always near water.

A few days later, from a campsite on the Mitchell River, Al and I hiked to the falls. It took us several hours, and we passed not a soul on the way. Close to our destination we discovered more evidence of an ancient Aboriginal presence, a spectacular burial platform jotted with sandstone cairns, overlooking a shimmering plain. We descended by rope over the main falls, not only testing my nerves, but spooking scores of roosting bats who had taken shelter in the dark recess behind the waterfall.

That night we caught some good size fish, sooty grunter, from the rock pools above the falls and camped out on the spinifex and warm boulders. In the waterhole we cooled the last of the wine we had bought on our way up through the Barossa Valley in South Australia. Next morning I discovered that while we slept something – native bush rats or a feral cat? – had knocked off several fish we left hanging in a calico bag less than a metre from our swags.

By now, the build-up to the Wet had begun. We needed to be off the rough bush tracks in case an early downpour cut the roads, so we set off south down the Gibb River Road, headed for Broome. Al and I had the romantic notion that we might hire an old pearling lugger there, and go exploring the remote northwest coast.

Our last camp was at Tunnel Creek, a cave above a watercourse that was home to freshwater crocodiles, thousands of flying foxes, and a slice of Australia's early bloody European history. In the late nineteenth century the cave had been the base of Jandamarra, or 'Pigeon', an outlaw to some, a freedom-fighter to others, who had waged guerilla war against police and settlers. He used Tunnel Creek as his hideout, disappearing without trace when police pursued him to the mouth of the cave. His pursuers failed to realise that there was a breach in the cave roof, through which the warrior escaped to the bluff above. His campaign ended in a shootout at Tunnel Creek in 1897, when he was hunted down and killed by a black tracker.

It was a powerful story which I had never heard before. Refuelling the Land Rover in Derby before the drive south, we learnt that Jandamarra's family had descendants living there. As I was learning, history always lay close at hand in the Kimberley. And so we drove the last leg to Broome, simply looking for a good time, or so I thought. I didn't realise then that this amazing frontier with its rich experience of human struggle and its wild red and blue beauty already had me like a fish on the end of a line, and that I would spend the best part of my twenties there.

CHAPTER 2

Broome

The road from Derby to Broome is all west or south-west, a final hurdle for hot, tired travellers coming off the Gibb River Road at the end of the day. After you cross the Fitzroy River at Willare, the drive is through monotonous cattle country, flat red-sand plains covered in dusty tropical scrub and gouged by wash-outs and creeks running red with sediment. As Al and I speared down Broome Road toward the old pearling town, the sun poured in through the dusty windscreen, almost blinding us.

It was late afternoon when we finally arrived, so instead of turning left to Broome, we turned right to Cable Beach, five kilometres away on the other side of the peninsula, making it to that long, wide highway of sand just in time to join the tourists, hippies, four-wheel drivers and local kids who congregate there to watch the sun go down in an orange blaze. By the late seventies, Cable Beach had become something of a 'scene', a must-do item on the itinerary of footloose younger travellers in the know, like Byron Bay on the east coast, or Kuta in Bali. As we had driven further into western Kimberley, every traveller of our own age that we met coming the other way was keen to tell us about Cable Beach.

Accommodation which was cheap or, even better, free was as hard to find in Broome then as it is now. We set up camp in the dunes behind the beach, like the other squatter groups availing themselves of some of Broome's best real estate. Soon, however, the presence of patrolling rangers forced us to move to the Bali Hai caravan park, a Broome landmark long since converted to the swank Cable Beach Club. In its raffish surroundings, amid a friendly community of long-term residents and travellers like ourselves, we pitched our tents.

It was Sunday night and there seemed to be almost nowhere open to eat. Eventually we settled for long soup at Tang Wei's Chinese restaurant, a café suffused in unnatural yellow-green fluorescent light. A teenage girl with long straight black hair and Aboriginal features served us, then vanished. A staticky Chinese language radio program played in the rear of the café. Apart from a drunk who came in for a takeaway, we were the only customers.

In stark contrast to the eerie quiet at Tang Wei's, the Roebuck Bay Hotel just around the corner was going off. Inside, the sweaty dance floor was packed shoulder to shoulder with locals and tourists, while an indigenous band pumped out heavily amplified rock and blues. Outside, two burly constables were trying to stuff an inebriated drinker into the back of a paddy wagon. The bloke was still calling for his dog from the caged van as the police drove away.

As we soon found out, Sundays seldom failed to deliver 'The Roey' a rowdy crowd of heroic drinkers. Its eclectic mix of patrons included lugger crews, meat workers, offshore drillers, survey crews, ringers, station hands, alternative lifestylers, and travellers. The pub was the focus of a thriving live music scene, and the Sunday afternoon session in particular offered punters a chance to blow off steam.

Drinks had been served at this location since 1890. Like many older buildings in town, The Roey's façade was dominated by its large corrugated iron roof, like a high-crowned hat pulled down low over the ears to keep the brain cool. Above an untidy fringe of red-sand footpath its wide front verandah looked out to a fringe of mangrove and the occasional glimpse of Roebuck Bay. Welcoming timber saloon doors swung open to reveal a roomy front bar where you could enjoy a jug of beer for about $5.

There were three other pubs in town but to my mind none had the mystique of The Roey, which was the pearlers' pub. In the heart of Chinatown, only a few minutes walk down the road from Streeters Jetty where the luggers still unloaded their pearl shell and took on fresh stores and fuel, it was the perfect watering hole, unpretentious yet directly connected to its romantic past, close to the workshops and chandlery sheds that had serviced the pearlers for decades.

Broome's pearling industry was then almost a century old, but it still revolved around the harvest of pearl shell just as it had in the beginning. In the days before plastic, the shell was used for making buttons, costume jewellery and combs. It was now exploited for other purposes as well, including the seeding of cultivated pearls.

Just as the colonial gold rushes had encouraged a flood of prospectors, so the discovery of rich beds of shell in waters off Broome attracted men by their thousands. At first they mainly came from Darwin, Thursday Island, Shark Bay, and Cossack at the mouth of the Harding River, where luggers put out to exploit rich beds of wild shell around Flying Foam Passage and deepwater beds off the Monte Bellos and Barrow Island.

By the industry's heyday in the 1890s more than three hundred luggers worked out of Roebuck Bay, harvesting the beds and cleaning the shell for export overseas. Eighty per cent of the world's mother-of-pearl, the shiny inner layer of the shell, came from the region, and Broome was as familiar a port of call for the master mariners of the day as Sydney or Singapore.

Lugger crews also found natural pearls, by law usually the property of the pearling master. Depending on their lustre, size and shape, such pearls were highly desirable and sometimes immensely valuable. In the old days before radio communication, skippers tended to closely guard their pearl finds for fear of mutiny among their crew. Luggers would simply disappear, and those aboard were never seen again. In one infamous case in 1899, the crew of the *Ethel* murdered its captain, Riddell, as well as his son and the first mate, then sailed the schooner to Koepang and scuttled it.

In this part of Australia the tides are among the biggest in the world, with movements of up to nine metres. At first, the vast shoreline exposed by low tide made shell collection easy. Local Aboriginal people provided a ready source of cheap expendable labour, press-ganged, coerced or otherwise lured into collecting wild pearl shell lying within the tide line.

By the early 1870s, 350 Aboriginal males were officially listed as working for seventy-five pearling masters off the northwest coast. Once the shell on the tidal flats was exhausted, boats were used to take groups of young Aboriginal men and women to free-dive and grope in the sandy mud of the bottom. If no shell was brought to the surface, the 'skin' or 'bare pelt' diver was obliged to produce a handful of mud to prove that he was not shirking.

During the following decades, pearling masters imported indentured workers from Asia and the Pacific Islands. A further wave of immigration before World War I would bring a steady influx of people from the Dodecanese islands off Greece, seeking to escape poverty and conflict. But the Broome of today really has its origins in the arrival of the Filipinos (or 'Manilamen', as they were known), Ceylonese, Timorese ('Koepangers'), Singaporeans and Indonesians ('Malays') and, last but not least, the Japanese, who soon gained a reputation for special prowess as divers.

After Australian nationhood in 1901, Asian entry was severely restricted by the White Australia policy. Nevertheless, labour migration from Japan to the pearling ports increased steadily, an early indication of the industry's political influence. The Chinese were just as important in their way. Not all arrived on Australian shores as indentured labourers; many came under their own steam during the gold rushes of the nineteenth century. In Broome, they established general stores, cafés and tailoring businesses. Tailor shops like Dep's specialised as suppliers to the pearling industry making 'pearlers whites' and woollen undergarments for the divers. The restaurant where Al and I ate that first night belonged to a family with a Chinese patriarch whose story was in some ways the story of Broome.

Tang Wei came to Broome in the late twenties, working his way as a crewman on a steamer from Hong Kong. He became a hard-hat diver, a very good one, and was promoted to head diver. He met and married Lexie D'Antoine, a Bardi Aboriginal woman of mixed European descent who had been born at Hunters Creek on the Dampier Peninsula. In the face of the legal restrictions on intermarriage, as well as opposition from local representatives of the Church, the couple bravely decided to travel to Perth where it was easier for them to marry. In the 1950s, Tang Wei opened his café to help support his growing family. Even then, the law restricted him from owning land, so a white pearling master helped him acquire his business, a common practice that benefited both parties.

By the late 1970s when I arrived in Broome, the White Australia Policy was gone for good, but only just. With its corrugated iron buildings and unfenced lots, Chinatown still had a makeshift air, as if its occupants did not really expect to be allowed to stay permanently. None of the stores and cafés had yet been self-consciously smartened up, and it would be some years before mass tourism disrupted the distinctive character and rhythm of Broome life. The elderly Chinese manager of L.L. Tack's general store still used an abacus to calculate the cost of a pair of thongs or a tee shirt. And every day at noon, as the heat and humidity grew oppressive, the entire quarter gratefully closed down for a two-hour siesta.

❋ ❋ ❋

AT THE end of Dampier Terrace, the dilapidated structure of Streeters Jetty extended about seventy metres out into a channel cut though the thick mangroves lining the Dampier Creek foreshore. Alongside this old pier two wooden-hulled pearling luggers were moored. They were flopped over at angles, temporarily beached by the receding tide on a foetid mud bank over which little red crabs competed with the resident mud skippers in search of food.

Nearby was an old Japanese divers' quarters, with a brass diving helmet hanging in its picturesque entrance, a wooden arch festooned with pink bougainvillea. A rough driveway continued along the foreshore leading to a covered slipway and chandlers on one side and more accommodation. A strong scent of frangipani emanated from nearby gardens.

It was mid-afternoon and no one was stirring, except for Al and me. We waited patiently for the premises of Streeter and Male, pearling masters, to reopen. The building in which the company was housed was a showpiece of interwar vernacular tropical architecture, with white-washed walls, corrugated iron roof, and a wide shaded verandah set on white ant-resistant concrete stumps.

Inside, the office appeared deserted. Behind a large solid timber counter lay a clutter of accounts, as if the staff had all left suddenly. The only sign of occupation was the ancient ceiling fan that creaked overhead, its blistered steel paddles stirring a barely detectable breeze.

Eventually someone emerged from one of the back rooms, a middle-aged man with a florid complexion which contrasted with the immaculate pearlers whites he wore. This was Kim Male, manager of the luggers we had seen down at the jetty. It took him just a few minutes to disabuse us of our plan to go to sea. There were fewer operational luggers than we had realised, just four these days, he told us, and they had finished their fishing contracts and were either slipped for repairs or had been decommissioned for the wet season. Even if they were still seaworthy, the cost of chartering one with a crew would be well beyond our budget.

So for Al and me it was back to the Bali Hai caravan park, where we pondered the depressing state of our finances. Our situation was becoming urgent.

One afternoon, after a swim at Cable Beach, Al got talking to a young couple travelling in a modified bus. 'Spud' was a bricklayer and had been offered a contract to build a new accommodation wing at the Tropicana motel. It was one of the first indications that the historic old town had a future in tourism. Spud needed help to finish the job before the Wet, and Al agreed to help. I would be the third leg of the team as builder's labourer, mixing concrete, fixing scaffold and stacking bricks.

The great advantage of the job was that we could leave our tents and move into one of the existing motel units that had been vacated during the work – sheer luxury. With the main block-laying complete, work focused on cleaning and fitting out the units. We were joined by another helper, Russell Massey.

Russell was like us, recently arrived in Broome from Melbourne, and willing to turn his hand to pretty much whatever work came along. He and his heavily pregnant Italian girlfriend, Francesca, were living in a rented caravan on Broome's industrial estate. We became frequent guests at his caravan and passed many pleasant evenings there listening to Rodriguez cassettes over cold beers and joints.

Work on the building site was coming to an end, and along with it my free accommodation. There was more bricklaying work available for Al, but for me it was no more job and no more bed. After a short stint camping at Russ's industrial block, where I spent several uncomfortable nights in a sleeping bag on a couple of wooden pallets in a sweltering tool shed, my luck took a turn for the better.

A place came up at Bishop's Palace, a historic boarding house in the centre of town, a favoured resort of hitchhikers, single working men, and others looking for affordable accommodation. This sprawling, single-storey timber residence had been built around the turn of the twentieth century by a wealthy pearling master. For many years it was used as a residence by the Anglican Bishop of Broome.

The Palace made up in atmosphere what it lacked in modern amenities. Set in an old garden, it faced seawards and caught the ocean breeze with a wide wrap-around verandah trimmed with wrought-iron lace. The interior was a dark rabbit warren of bedrooms, rust-stained bathrooms, and a cockroach-infested communal kitchen. Several semi-detached tropical bungalows clung to the back of the building, extending the accommodation. I was assigned a room in one of them. It was powered, had a fan, an old iron bed frame and mattress – luxury, compared with my recent circumstances.

The neighbours were interesting too. The first night that I slept there I was woken at dawn by the noise of a large truck pulling up outside. The driver alighted and came to a door near mine, rasping out a demand: 'Hey, you got any coldies in there? Give me one.'

A woman's voice from inside moaned an inaudible reply. The creak of a wire screen door was followed a moment later by the hiss of a beer can being opened. The truck's engine fired up and the driver departed as quickly as he had arrived.

The Palace provided me with my entrée to the pearling industry.

Late one oppressively hot afternoon I was lying on my single bed under the small fan. Somewhere nearby I heard what I thought was the sound of a banjo. Someone was playing simple chords from the theme of the movie *Deliverance*. I heaved myself off the bed and went to investigate. The novice banjo player was sitting on the wide back stairs of the main house, plucking and strumming determinedly while a mate looked on. Broome was a town full of young people, but the youth of this pair of adventurers was striking.

Steve Arrow, the banjo player, introduced himself. He was just nineteen, the son of a Koorda wheat farmer, and had decided to come to Broome after reading about its pearling luggers. He had driven up from Perth in an old roofless Land Rover with his cattle dog, Beau, for company. He told me his vehicle's battery had been so flat that at night he left the car running while he camped by the roadside. Steve's friend Drew Bessen was the son of a Perth accountant, and an excellent free diver.

When they weren't working they liked to spear fish around the wharf pilings at Broome jetty. Both blokes were superbly fit and naturally competitive, often daring each other to see who could dive deepest around the wharf, skills which would be put to good use when the pearling season began in earnest. Steve had had the good fortune to hook up with Bruce Farley, a pearling contractor who had bought a decommissioned PPL fleet lugger and started his own pearling venture. Though the diving season was finished, Farley had other work to finish before the onset of the Wet. This was good news for me because he needed some casual hired help. I was offered a fortnight's work, my first on a Broome pearling lugger.

CHAPTER 3

Lugger buggers

The waters off Broome produce South Sea pearls, some of the biggest and most beautiful pearls in the world. The shell which produces them belongs to the *Pinctada Maxima* (large pearl oyster). It's a handsome thing in its way, growing up to a foot long in the old measure, with a silver or golden lip.

A cultured pearl takes about eighteen months to mature inside one of these shells. When it is harvested, that is not the end of the shell's usefulness. Kept alive, it can be used to grow blister pearls for jewellery-making. After a further eighteen months these blisters are drilled out, and the remnant hull of the pearl shell cleaned and packed for sale. My job was to help with this cleaning and packing.

Farley's lugger, the *DMcD*, was anchored on his pearl farm about seven kilometres offshore from Broome. The farm was a leased area of hard sea bottom identified at the surface by buoys, where wild pearl shell fished from other areas was rested before and after seeding.

The work was carried out on the lugger's crowded decks; it was hot, monotonous and tiring. A team of divers brought up reseeded shell for harvesting. It was chopped open, the muscle and guts removed and the shell halves scrubbed clean and packed. The blister pearls would be drilled out later onshore.

The divers also retrieved dump bags full of shell which had been rested and was ready for reseeding. Steve and I cleaned it, then deposited the shell inside wire baskets in a tank pump-fed with fresh sea water. This storage kept shell alive until the semi-circular plastic beads used for growing half-pearls was inserted.

The operation took a fortnight and was not all hard yakka. During lunch breaks we would go for a swim to cool off, climbing the ratlines and diving in. Free-diving was encouraged, partly because Farley was always on the lookout for fresh diving talent. 'If you're a good pearl diver, you've got to be a good free diver,' he would tell us. We often activated the lugger's depth sounder to measure our skill.

I remember Drew Bessen having little difficulty reaching a depth of 30 metres, while I was lucky if I could manage 20. It was during one of these lunchtime sessions that I first tried out the divers' breathing apparatus. I was keen to progress to diving, like Drew and Steve, if I could make the grade. It seemed a good life to me.

THE LAST PEARLING LUGGER

The divers would sometimes spear a fish for lunch or dinner. At night after a few beers or ciders, we pulled some wire shell baskets together and threw our foam mattresses on top, lying under the stars on a calm sea with the lights of Broome twinkling in the distance.

On this trip we were lucky with the weather. We had finished the job before a warning was issued that a tropical low north of Broome was headed our way. The *DMcD* scarpered back to port. Farley took no chances, driving the lugger up Dampier Creek, where we tied her up in the mangroves to wait out the storm.

Al and I headed back to Melbourne for Christmas, agreeing to return in the new year. Before we departed, hitching a lift down to Perth on a road train, I collected my pay and sounded out Farley about a deckhand's job. No luck there: he had a full crew already for the next season. It was some compensation that he told me I had worked well, and he would keep me in mind if a vacancy came up.

*   *   *

WHEN I returned to Broome, another room had become vacant at the Palace and I wasted no time in claiming it, a prime corner bedroom in the main building, with a large bougainvillea growing right outside the shuttered window. One of its sinuous branches had begun snaking its way into my room; room service being what it was at the Palace, over the coming months I was able to monitor its steady advance.

I was still hanging out for a job on a lugger, but by 1979 the fleet had become quite small, just as Kim Male had said when we visited his office. Locally, there were the four luggers owned by Pearls Pty Ltd (PPL), the international cultured pearl syndicate with which Male's firm was associated, and, in addition, the single-boat operations of Dick Morgan and Farley. So the season was well underway before an opportunity arrived in the unlikely guise of a killer hangover.

It is quite possible that I would never have found the opening I was looking for if I hadn't gotten drunk one night with Lal, the *DMcD*'s deckhand and spare diver. Lal was a character, always game for something. Perhaps his most memorable exploit was the time (a few years later) that he decided to keep an old Broome tradition alive by having pearls inserted in his foreskin.

The Japanese divers who still practised this custom believed that pearls under the foreskin enhanced the experience of intercourse. All Lal's friends who had had the operation performed spoke warmly of the results: no doubt they had to justify the massive expense somehow.

Normally the delicate procedure was performed by someone who had the skills of a surgeon and equipment to match, but not in Lal's case. As one of his crewmates told me later: 'We got Lal and put his dick on the galley chopping block. Then we got the pearls "in" using the ship's (nautical) dividers. Bang! Just like that.'

Sadly for Lal, the episode ended with an infection that put him in hospital. After this near-death experience he retired from active service on the pearling luggers.

But back to that famous evening in 1979, when Lal and I went out on a spree. The *DMcD* was due to sail on the tide, around daybreak, and Lal was supposed to have been at Town Beach for the early morning departure. Instead, by his own account, he woke up in a drain somewhere between the Roebuck Bay Hotel and Bishop's Palace.

I was not feeling much better, but at least I had managed to stagger back to my room after the party broke up in the wee hours. Nursing a gale force hangover, I shuffled over to the Continental Hotel late the next morning to seek solace in an air-conditioned lounge and chill my fevered brain, thankful that the fleet had left for another ten days, and that my liver would have a chance to recover.

I had just ordered my first life restoring beer when a vaguely familiar voice interrupted my daydream: 'Dodd – you still want that job on a lugger?' It was Farley, standing in the doorway with a deep furrowed scowl on his face, examining me furiously through the glasses perched on his beaklike nose. Not waiting for an answer, he snapped: 'You've got ten minutes to grab your gear. I'll pick you up outside the Palace.'

Bolting down my drink and waiving rights to my lunch order, I dashed across Bedford Park back to my room. It was a scorcher of a day, and the sudden exertion felt like a near death experience. Rivulets of sweat gushed from my pores, falling in big fat droplets onto the bed as I packed a basic survival kit for a week or more at sea.

Into an old sports bag I threw a floppy hat, sheets, a spare pair of shorts, a shower bag, my Reef sun tan oil and a tube of sun block, and, as an afterthought, my favourite Leo Kottke cassette.

Farley was already parked outside the Palace in a rust-streaked Suzuki four-wheel drive. A dinghy was waiting for us at Town Beach. We were soon hurtling across turquoise water toward the *DMcD*, my hangover soaking up each blast of saltwater spray as we slammed across a gentle swell.

Manoeuvring alongside the lugger, the driver of the dinghy cut the engine, and the dinghy was heaved aboard by willing hands hauled up onto the fore deck, and lashed down. Taking wobbly steps along the wet wooden deck I found a seat on the engine room hatch to contemplate the consequences of my apparent good luck in getting the job.

I felt very guilty about Lal's sudden demise, but there was little time for moral philosophy as the *DMcD* picked up speed, punching into a brisk south-easterly. In open water past Gantheaume Point, the entrance to Roebuck Bay, the lugger began what seemed to me like a death roll. We changed course southwest for the pearling grounds, crashing through an endless bank of stomach-churning swells.

I was soon down on all fours, seasickness doubling me over. I groped my way to the gunwale just in time to avoid throwing up all over the deck, much to the amusement of my crewmates. But there was work to be done. The first order I received was to go below and put the kettle on, to make tea for the crew. Entering the forward hatch to the galley, I nearly fell headlong down the wooden ladder as the boat pitched and rolled. Steve Arrow and the head deckhand, Mark Feeney, hoisted the jib sail, which helped stabilise the lugger and lessen its roll.

The *DMcD*, like most of the other luggers operating out of Broome, still carried sail. She had been built in 1957 by Kevin Buckeridge, a master shipwright from Fremantle who had been coaxed north. Constructed at Scotts' slipway in Broome, she was 52 feet from stem to stern and 26 tonnes, jarrah-planked with laminated frames. Her knees and engine bed were hacked from local cadjebut, a bush timber cut from Barred Creek north of Broome.

She was named for Daniel McDaniel, one of Broome's pioneering pearlers, and had been commissioned by Male and Co, then one of Broome's oldest pearling concerns. In the early seventies, Male and Co began a series of alterations to its fleet, raising the foredecks of the luggers to enlarge the accommodation for the new generation of divers, many of them former abalone divers from South Australia. They were physically bigger than most of their Asian counterparts, and more demanding in terms of onboard living conditions. During this refit, the *DMcD* was given a new keel, ribs, planks and decking.

The engines were also upgraded, and the sails became ancillary. Although the *DMcD* retained her sails, over time her masts were shortened. The jib was still useful if a stiff south-easterly was blowing. Farley reckoned he got an extra knot with all the sails up and the engine running. That would have given her a top speed of just over seven knots: she was definitely no ocean greyhound.

She had a minimal electronic fit-out, a 60-nautical-mile radar, VHF radio, depth sounder and auto helm wired into a small exposed console at the stern. Forward of the engine room, set into the deck, was a steel tank capable of holding more than two thousand live pearl shell stored in wire baskets. The water in the tank helped act as ballast, particularly on some memorable return journeys when every conceivable space including the galley and engine room was taken up with bags of pearl shell.

Accommodation was sparse: four single bunks in the forward galley compartment, double-stacked port and starboard, with a fifth for emergencies butted across the chain anchor locker.

In the stern compartment there were three berths, two singles port and starboard, and a third tucked across the beam just forward of the steering gear. The engine room was squeezed in amidships, where there was just enough space for the main propulsion unit, a reliable old Volvo Penta, sundry pumps, filters and an air compressor tank.

The top bunks in the forward compartment were coveted because they were positioned under a ventilator which could be adjusted topside to direct gusts of cool fresh air. There was a knack to using them. When the lugger's bow was pointed into rough seas that cool breeze could turn just as suddenly into a Niagara Falls of salt water.

As a lowly ranked deckhand, I had last choice of berth and was directed to the lower starboard rack in the forward galley compartment. On my first night, a cockroach scurried over me as I lay sweltering on top of my mattress hoping for sleep that never came. Cockroaches and rats were an age-old problem on the luggers. Before the advent of insect sprays, skippers would beach their boats and let the tide literally wash them out.

Our roach problem wasn't helped by the fact that the chest freezer in the galley was always breaking down. Fresh meat and vegetables would last about three days, bread about five, before acquiring a range of mould types that would not have looked out of place in Saddam Hussein's germ lab. Near the end of each fishing trip, the freezer would inevitably fail due to constant opening and shutting of its door and the rocking motion of the lugger. The result was a slurry of decomposing food slopping around in the bottom of the unit, which defied our constant efforts to keep it clean.

After the cockroach incident I stayed below deck as a last resort. Except when it was raining, I dragged my mattress upstairs and camped under the stars. My fellow crew members in the forward compartment would probably say I had no choice in the matter because of my snoring. But give me a night under the heavens, a balmy breeze and the gentle rocking of a lugger as a panacea for any form of sleeplessness.

Well, almost. On more than a few mornings I woke in pitch darkness under a howling gale. My sheets had blown away to Port Hedland and I'd be lying stark naked clinging on to the mattress for dear life. Ask any crewman. On a lugger, sleep is as hard to come by as dry bedding.

* * *

MANY HAVE heard the alluring call of life on a pearling lugger, but for a few it turns out to be a siren song. I remember one bloke we called Bob Blob-a-job, who most certainly should never have gone to sea on the *DMcD*. I met him at the Palace, and he pestered me, Steve and Drew for months, asking if he could come out for a trip and savour the 'lugger experience'.

Never have I seen anyone as seasick as poor old Bob proved to be, still unable to stand on his feet at the end of the first day. He lay slumped on the deck for hours, his arms gripped tight around the base of the mizzen. Hard bastards that we were, we showed little compassion for his plight.

By the time evening fell and dinner was served, his large, overweight frame was still sprawled out on the stern, its owner moaning and dry-retching. His demeanour was hardly improved when Steve bent down beside him and waved a bowl of steaming beef curry under his nose, before slurping up the gravy with gusto.

Thereafter, Blob-a-job spent most of the trip in his bunk, emerging from time to time for a recuperative nap on the foredeck. As days passed, he earnt our enmity and, ultimately, our disgust because it seemed to us he was unwilling to even try helping us with our huge workload. He had given up.

Whenever my own suitability for lugger life was rudely questioned by my more experienced crewmates (one of my several nicknames was Dodderer – not entirely fair!), I could remind them that seafaring was in my genes. An uncle who was a merchant marine had served as a senior captain with the Harrison Line. During World War II he survived two sinkings courtesy of German U-boats, and earnt the George Cross for his exploits on wartime supply convoys to Russia. I was not so keen to invoke the distant relative who had been chief engineer on the RMS *Titanic*.

Those of us who made the grade on the luggers were mostly attracted to pearling by the healthy, freewheeling lifestyle but also the prospect of better than average money. The skipper and owner of the *DMcD*, Farley, was a former abalone diver and keen spear fisherman who hailed from South Australia. He had worked on barges in the Gulf of Carpentaria before he moved to Broome in the early seventies, and began work as a driver and diver for PPL. He was one of the first to take on the Japanese by adapting the technology used by the abalone divers to pearling. The results revolutionised the industry. In the early seventies, when the so-called 'white divers' took over, they could earn up to $70,000 a year if they were good, comparable to the rich wages skilled workers can now earn in the mining industry.

Farley would reward initiative, and was unafraid of breaking the mould to try new ideas or fishing tactics. That alone distinguished him from many of his former colleagues at PPL. He often came across as aloof and arrogant, and was notoriously short tempered. Yet he was also fair. I had some frightful arguments with him, but they usually blew over quickly with no recrimination. In later months I felt he was miserly about wages, but I couldn't help but admire him as an innovator, a risk taker and a competent skipper.

We all had nicknames, and in that first season I was out on the *DMcD*, he was the subject of several. First he was Fearless as in Fearless Farley. Then he became Frog Shit or sometimes Fearless Frog Shit. The tag which eventually stuck was The Creature derived from Stick Creature, a reference to his tall lean frame.

The Creature had a penchant for sleeping naked on his bunk bed, a habit which led to much idle speculation among the crew about the size of his equipment. Big Bag Barker, who would have known, because he shared the stern quarters with the skipper for a couple of seasons, claimed that Farley had a fourteen-inch prick.

At thirty-six, Bruce Barker was the oldest member of the crew. A big, barrel-chested former shearer with a shock of blond hair, Barker had acquired his nickname because he reminded us all of the heavy-duty dump bags we used for shell fishing. Tough as nails, he had a dry sense of humour, the legacy of a life on outback stations. He had only begun working the luggers in 1978, but his competence was clear. He was the sort of naturally able yet self-deprecating bloke who was not only good company but handy in a crisis.

Unlike the other crew Barker was not much of a reader. While we devoured books in our spare time Big Bag would usually read a few lines from his favourite, the *Divers' Medical Handbook*, before falling asleep with the manual flopped over his chest. He claimed it was one of only three books he had ever read in his life, the others being the violent thriller *The Dogs of War* and the Victorian adventure classic *King Solomon's Mines*. Creature comforts meant little to Big Bag. More than one night he went to sleep wearing his wetsuit pants so he could be up and at it first thing in the morning.

Burly John Stewart was head diver. Affable and easy going, a chain smoker who always seemed to be fiddling with a cigarette, John was a romantic, constantly scanning industry magazines for his dream boat. We dubbed him 'The Colonel' for his old-fashioned mannerisms. He had a rather inflated opinion of his singing talents and once threatened to entertain us with a self-penned dirge entitled 'Down to the Eighty Mile', which he planned to perform during a Sunday session at the Roey, splicing rope while he sang. He reconsidered after Barker threatened his own form of entertainment – a live strangulation.

I remembered the Colonel telling me how he never actually swam when pearl fishing, but hopped like a kangaroo along the bottom as he picked up shell. To prove his point he cut the ends of his black flippers, saying they were not needed for propulsion but only to balance on as he pirouetted along the ocean floor. But his approach was not universally shared, and this might explain why he had the lowest shell count on the *DMcD*, even though he was head diver.

At times, the Colonel's helmsmanship was called into question. Once he was on watch on the return trip to Broome when for some reason best known to himself he activated the lugger's weather helm. Normally this helm was used to compensate the steering in the event of a strong easterly blowing.

While the Colonel popped down to the galley to make a brew, Farley came up on deck for a piss. 'He's hanging his huge slug overboard to cool it off when he sees the lugger heading straight for the rocks off Cape Bossut,' Big Bag told me later. There was no wind, and the lugger had nosed to starboard.

'"Fuck, what's going on here", he yells. The Colonel stumbles back on deck trying to explain how he set the weather helm unaware it would cause the boat to veer off course. The Creature responds with a blast of abuse. "You useless bastard!"'

The head deckhand was Mark Feeney, who in the off season worked as a cray fisherman. He was in his late twenties, married, with two young children and plenty of responsibilities, and at the end of pearling season he would dash south to Geraldton and the other fleet.

He came with a reputation as someone who was not shy for a scrap, having emerged victorious in several bouts of fisticuffs among the cray crews, but like Barker he was a laid-back sort of bloke, with an acid wit and a laconic turn of phrase. With a roll-your-own smoke always hanging off his lip, Feeney was an uncomplaining hard worker whose seamanship was second to none.

Both Feeney and Barker were already seasoned fishermen and would go on to acquire their skippers tickets. As for the rest of the crew, Drew (Droopy) Bessen had one season as a diver under his belt, while Steve Arrow (dubbed Squire, because his family was on the land) was spare diver as well as deckhand.

While I soon found my sea legs, I never overcame my dread of waking to face another working day on the *DMcD*. Inevitably, my sleep would be shattered by the noise of someone tinkering in the engine room, checking oil and bilge levels. The tinkering was followed by a deafening racket of a wrench being struck against the engine block – Farley's way of rousing the crew. The Volvo Penta diesel would be cranked over, my cue for another diving day.

After inspecting the cramped engine room, Farley would descend the wooden stairs leading to our forward galley compartment to put on the kettle. It was usually still dark with just a hint of dawn over the land when we hit the deck. Our first job was to lift the anchor. It took a sharp eye to point the helmsman in the direction of the lay of chain as we came up on the pick.

We had an electric winch but it didn't much like salt water, so often we found ourselves winding up the anchor by hand. In deep water – 120 feet – we came up with a novel retrieval method. Someone would dive down and attach an airbag to the anchor, and pump it full of compressed air from our regulators while two crewmen wound furiously by hand to take up the chain as the anchor came off the bottom. At first the anchor gained momentum slowly, but by the time it got near the surface it was travelling at the speed of a submarine-launched ballistic missile.

Hand-winching was character-building when the weather was fine. Faced into a southwest gale with the bow bouncing up and down like a berserk beast and Farley screaming inaudible orders at us from the helm, it always reminded me of a chaotic scene from *Moby Dick*. All that was missing was the whale.

At last, with the anchor raised and tied off, the *DMcD* was ready for diving operations.

CHAPTER 4

The stuffer patches

The best conditions for diving occur during what are called neap tides, when the gravitational force exerted on the sea by the sun and moon is weakest. The result is less disturbance of the sea bottom and optimal underwater visibility.

Following the long tradition of the pearling fleet, we fished neaps and returned home on the spring tides, when the gravitational disturbance of the water was strongest. This meant we were in and out of port about twice a month. Off the northwest coast of Australia a neap tide cycle varies from about four to ten days or even more, enough time to put to sea and get a decent dive in.

If the difference between the neap and spring tides was minimal and conditions were fine, some boats might stay on the grounds fishing two neaps. But this was rare, because the luggers needed to be refuelled and reprovisioned – as did the divers. At the end of a neap, the *DMcD* would usually turn back to Broome where, after unloading and packing the cleaned pearl shell we had on board, we would repair to the Roebuck Bay Hotel.

During those early neaps of '79, the PPL fleet used to anchor fairly close together. In the distance we could make out their luggers by their twinkling mast lights, two boats skippered by Japanese, the other two by a pair of Australians who were ferocious rivals. I had some good friends on those boats: Richard Baillieu, known by everyone as Salty Dog or Salty, and Wayne House (Wonder Dog). Wayne was a middle-class lad from Perth who had been a schoolboy swimming champion. He eventually brought half his friends up with him to Broome. Salty was the sprig of a family of Melbourne blueblood and an ex-Geelong Grammar boy – not that he'd let that prevent him from leading a rover's life. He had been a ringer on cattle stations and worked in the remote northwest for diamond exploration companies, but had also run nightclubs, and at one stage was bar manager at the Roebuck Bay Hotel. It was Farley who had offered him his first job as a diver, after he cadged his first go at diving on a PPL boat of which The Creature was then skipper.

Though there was strong camaraderie between the crews, competition between boats for the best catch rate was intense. The PPL luggers even had their own code they used when they reported in by radio each evening to their mother ship. Not that it helped much because we broke the code, thanks to an indiscreet employee no doubt induced to reveal all after a Roey drinking session.

There was also the *Paspaley I*, a modified fibreglass tuna boat, 27 metres, Japanese-built, and luxuriously fitted out compared with the rest of the boats. She used to motor down from Darwin, where the Paspaley interests were based. Even if we were unable to see her we could certainly hear her, the noise of the diesel auxiliary engine reverberating across the water and disturbing the tranquillity of an otherwise peaceful night at sea.

The Paspaley story was a remarkable tale of persistence and initiative. Nicholas Paspaley's family was among the exodus from the Greek islands during the upheaval in Europe around World War I. He arrived in Australia as a child in 1919, began work at fourteen, and within five years had purchased his first lugger. He had hung on through the bad times of the forties and early fifties, and was one of the first pearlers to sign a deal with the Japanese to cultivate cultured pearls.

While Broome-based PPL's joint venture with the Japanese entrepreneurs flourished, the Paspaley cultured pearl operation at Port Essington in the Northern Territory did not. The area had previously been heavily fished. It was closed down in 1969. Yet, by the late seventies the family had bounced back, putting to excellent use the pearl-seeding techniques they had learnt, and acquiring huge pearl farm leases in the Northern Territory, including some pristine waters off the Coburg Peninsula which produced very high quality pearls.

In 1979, Farley had a contract to fish about thirty thousand live shell for Paspaley, but since he had just started out he also took the opportunity to fish for mother-of-pearl for himself. He started the season in late March off Cape Bossut, south of Broome, venturing further south over consecutive trips as the weather grew more stable.

That was the fleet the season I started, save for occasional sightings of the Port Smith-based *Sea Venture*, a ferro-cement vessel owned by Dick Morgan. It had a mixed crew of Malays and Vietnamese and one very white diver, Mark Walsh, usually standing on the stern and easily identified by his flowing blond locks.

Like us, the *Sea Venture* was looking for mother-of-pearl. The boat was competition and when we were unable to get a visual sighting, we monitored its movement on our radar. If it remained in one area for long we would become suspicious and motor over to investigate if it had discovered good patches of wild shell. Morgan was an experienced pearler and commanded respect among the other skippers.

* * *

THE DIVING equipment that we used was known as the hookah system. Unlike self-contained scuba diving, it involved a compressor on deck pumping filtered air to the divers below. The air passed through hoses which were connected to a regulator or demand valve which allowed the diver to breathe at his own rate.

When I entered the industry, the hookah system had only recently replaced the traditional pearlers' hard-hat which had served the pearling industry for almost a century. It was very old technology. A German-born Englishman

THE LAST PEARLING LUGGER

Augustus Siebe, 'the Father of Diving', invented the first copper diving helmet in 1819. Spurred on by the pearling industry, his apparatus eventually evolved into the two-piece diving dress familiar to every boy who ever attended Saturday movie matinees. It comprised a sealable diving helmet with glass portals and rubberised canvas diving suit (one size fits all), and made the wearer look adventurous and alien at the same time.

In Broome, a diving revolution began in the early seventies when PPL hired a former naval officer called Peter Cummings to overhaul techniques until then dominated by Japanese stumbling across the ocean bottom in hard hat and lead boots. Word had spread about the success of new methods used by the abalone fishing industry, and Cummings soon recruited an abalone diver named Dale Chapman. Equipped with lightweight wetsuits, flippers and the hookah breathing apparatus Chapman and other young divers like Farley, Dave Dureau and Allan Badger quickly transformed the collection of wild pearl shell.

There were also far-reaching design changes to the PPL fleet that vastly improved the efficiency of shell collection. Alan Nunn, who had been a boilermaker in Newcastle, put his industrial expertise to good effect in steel outrigger booms which replaced the short stubby outriggers traditionally used by those on deck to feed out the heavy air hose to the hard-hat divers. The new outriggers allowed two or three divers at a time to be trawled along the bottom. It was a much more effective method than a single hard-hat diver, suspended from a stationary lugger, groping for shell on the ocean floor.

51

In the space of a few months, old rubber diving suits, brass hard hats, coils of heavy thick rubber air hose, lead boots, brass corselets, and woollen undergarments were gathering dust in the PPL warehouses next to the Streeters Jetty. I remember seeing the old gear still hanging up in the sheds when I signed on with the company in the early 1980s. By then the old hard-hats were valuable relics of another era, and many of them were eventually stolen.

At first, the Japanese poured scorn on the new methods. Their resistance lasted only until they witnessed firsthand the divers' shell catch. In 1971, diving in shallow 'asparagus country' near Manari north of Broome, Dureau took a thousand shell in a single day and Farley more than 1400, a record that has never been beaten.

The industry was infamous for its tough conditions. Kim Male's grandfather, Arthur, who started the family pearling business, was a feared figure in Broome at the turn of the twentieth century. His son Sam, who became PPL's managing director, also had a reputation as a hard taskmaster and a stickler for the rule book. He was a common sight in his pearlers whites, making the morning rounds, issuing orders to crew and employees and checking on the lugger fleet to ensure all was shipshape and Bristol fashion.

One morning the skipper of PPL's cargo boat MV *Broome* was summoned by the chief executive. 'Good morning, captain. I have to inform you that the tide has come up but your ship has not,' Sam Male said, referring to an accidental sinking. The fate of the hapless skipper goes unrecorded although the boat was raised and continued to provide a regular service.

THE LAST PEARLING LUGGER

It wasn't long before the white divers became aware of a big discrepancy in their wages and those paid to Asian crewmen, who received a pittance by comparison even though they were highly skilled. 'White deckies could chip shell and that was about it. The coloured crew had the boat skills and knew all about rigging and sailing,' Dureau told me.

The white divers threatened not to put to sea without equal pay for their crewmates.

PPL resisted the demand, then made an improved offer for the Asian crew most of whom were still hired as indentured labourers. It was this industrial dispute which also led to improved living conditions on the pearling luggers. Nevertheless, showers and toilets remained nonexistent. To relieve oneself meant a squat over the stern.

Though PPL had made concessions, Sam Male and its management were unimpressed, and took steps to ensure there would be no more industrial disputes. At the same time, this successful new generation of pearl divers demanded a bigger share of the profits. So pearl divers were put on share-fishing contracts and paid a catch rate per shell, usually higher for young shell suitable for cultured pearls.

Bruce Farley, by then a PPL skipper, was one of the first contractors who decided there was no longer a need for specialised professionals. Keen young men like Drew, Steve and me could be hired off the street and trained to dive for pearl shell.

* * *

It was either on my second or third trip down to the grounds that we broke away from the fleet. One evening we made our move with military precision, not wanting to alert the other boats.

We had had a day of slim pickings in shallow water off Mangrove Point, working what we called 'potato country' because the marine growth on the shell made the sea floor resemble a potato patch. This growth reduced visibility and obscured the shell, making it more difficult to discern.

Farley had been talking about a move south to another old shell ground near a place he called Three Sandhills. It had been weighing on his mind for a while. During the previous spring tide he had been busy checking old chart references with his friend Keith Carter, a PPL fleet engineer.

After dinner we washed up as normal but, instead of hitting the sack, we slipped our mooring and sailed south for several hours, the anchor lights of the other boats slowly fading into the distance. We dozed in our bunks waiting for the inevitable call from Farley to stand by the anchor.

When it came it was past midnight. The sea was calm and I was just happy to get back to sleep on the foredeck. The sun had barely risen when we raised the anchor to begin looking for productive shell bottom hopefully strewn with enough wild pearl shell to sustain several fishing neaps.

In the distance about six nautical miles to the east was the unmistakeable outline of three sandhills, the prominent feature on the Eighty Mile where the shoreline flattened out behind the encroaching expanse of the Great Sandy Desert.

THE LAST PEARLING LUGGER

At first, drifts over prospective ground yielded little shell. The Colonel prepared for another immersion. He stepped onto the starboard diving ladder, put on his flippers, face mask, purged his regulator and sank beneath the waves like a large seal, a stream of silvery air bubbles trailing in his wake.

After a few minutes elapsed he sounded one long blast on the signal horn – an encouraging sign. Then came a second blast. A shell patch had been found.

The Creature throttled back and, in preparation for action, dumped the drogue, a large heavy-duty sheet of sailcloth tethered to the stern bollard which acted as a sea anchor.

There was excitement on deck as we laid out the wet hessian mat on which we chopped the shell. We stood by to receive the shell bags, wooden chopping blocks prepared and axes and knives at the ready for the frenzy of cleaning that would follow.

The other divers suited up and joined the Colonel on the bottom. It was an amazing find for such a well fished area: a carpet of mostly mature shell which had lain untouched for years. Before the season finished we would fish more than a hundred tonnes of commercial shell, a record unheard of since the halcyon pre-war pearling days.

Over ensuing neaps we worked methodically, hoovering up the concentrated patches as we moved steadily south from the Three Sandhills. The patches appeared to lie in quite shallow waters, at a depth that varied from 45 feet at low tide to around 60 feet on the change.

Initially, the diving team comprised the Colonel diving directly off the stern behind the drogue, with Big Bag and Drew at port and starboard. Then the ever inventive Creature decided to try four divers, borrowing Steve Zimmerle and Kevin Piper from Paspaley to experiment. We settled into a four-diver routine, two port and two starboard, with Squire finally getting his wish granted and becoming the fourth diver.

A typical drift might last forty-five minutes. It depended on the depth of water and how much shell was lying on the bottom. Below, the divers emptied shell from their neck bags into their main work bag which was attached to a heavy duty yellow inflatable sack called a parachute. The bag holding the shell was clipped onto a weighted pulley system running off the outriggers. A work line ran off the weight which trailed about a metre off the bottom.

The diver held onto the rope line with one hand, and was towed along by the lugger picking up shell with his free hand. After receiving three tugs on their air line divers were expected to stop work and immediately begin their ascent, but there were many occasions when they delayed coming up, especially if they were on a good shell patch. We called it 'shopping after hours', and it was strongly discouraged in the interests of overall fairness. If a diver failed to abide by the rules and was a persistent offender then he was off the boat.

When it was time to surface the divers injected air from their regulators into the parachute sending their catch on its way to the surface while they ascended at a more leisurely pace, the deeper the water the more time for safe decompression.

Deckies used grappling hooks to pull the bags alongside the boat and either winch them up or physically heave them aboard. And now the real work began. Both divers and deckhands were paid per shell. After dump bags were emptied, the shell was counted and numbers recorded in the tally book, an anxious time for the divers as they compared scores. Nobody wanted to come last and competition underwater was deadly keen. Tussles over ownership of shell were not unknown, nor practices such as going under a colleague's work line to 'poach' shell.

The shell was not all that divers collected underwater. There was a ready market in Broome for cowrie and bailer shells, which were plundered from the ocean bottom in huge numbers. To this day the Eighty Mile suffers from the environmental devastation wreaked by my generation of shell seekers who stripped the bottom of decipians, a striking species of cowrie shell.

On deck while the lugger lined up on the patch again, the divers usually took a short break while the deck crew were hard at work chopping and scraping congealed growth off shell earmarked for cultivation. Sitting still and resting between dives was a precaution against the bends, but if it was very busy the divers jumped in to help clean shell, at least on the *DMcD*. In the early neaps it was just me, Feeney and Farley cleaning shell, but with Steve joining the divers it was quickly obvious a third deckhand was needed. Russell Massey who I had met earlier on the building site became the newest recruit.

By now, I was so familiar with the cleaning process that I could have probably performed it in my sleep. Our equipment was basic, a heavy duty butchers' chopper and a cheap stainless steel blade, usually part of some ancient cutlery set, its handle bound in a piece of old diving hose to ensure a good grip. After cleaning, the 'live shell' were placed into wire baskets and put into the storage tank to await transfer. That left the shell that was too old and wormy for cultivation, the big old molluscs known as 'clunkers' or 'commies' (commercial shell). They were harvested for mother-of-pearl, a practice known, predictably, as 'commie-bashing'.

The shells were scraped with a knife, the lip chopped to allow a knife to sever the muscle before the two halves were ripped apart. The gut was removed and put in a bucket; the opaque yellow muscle was cut off the shell and placed in a separate bin for washing before being strung out on a wire line to dry. It was a valuable by-catch, sold dried to some obscure Asian trader in Hong Kong where it fetched exorbitant prices as an aphrodisiac. Even the shell gut was sometimes used. We would drag it behind the lugger in hessian bags (often finding small baroque pearls in the process) and the constant churning would clean and tenderise it. Mixed with spices and vinegar and garlic, it was sold in old wine flagons to indigenous customers at the Continental Hotel.

The shell halves piled on deck were then scrubbed with a wire brush and blasted with the saltwater deck hose. For me this was the worst job, bent down on all fours working with a wire brush to remove the muscle remnants before blasting the shell with the water. The scrubbed shells were packed into hessian bags which were sewn up and stacked on the foredeck. For each shell collected I was paid the grand sum of six cents.

It was tedious, back-breaking work in the most literal sense, bearable when the weather was calm, but a bloody grim slog when conditions turned nasty. The hard jarrah deck was awash with shell grit which ground into your knees resulting in ugly sores. I spent valuable time patching up sores and cuts which festered with the constant exposure to grit, pearl guts and sea water.

The cleaning was never-ending, interspersed with the myriad other jobs that required attention on a working pearl lugger. Meals had to be prepared and hot water kept on the boil because the water temperature was still cold, and hot tea or coffee was usually served to the divers between every descent. There were tendering duties, regular checks to ensure that the divers' pulley weights were not dragging, that air hoses were not tangled, that the course heading was correct. The engine room also required frequent checking that everything was as it should be: bilge water, air compressor, engine temperature, oil pressure.

This sounds a well ordered routine but it was total mayhem once the divers hit a big patch and the deck was piled with shell. The deck had to be cleared before the divers surfaced again, and the whole process was repeated. Yet with so much shell coming up that was getting difficult. With every drift, we had to tally, clean, chop, sort and pack hundreds of shell.

But as the counts increased, keeping up became impossible, and we simply heaved the cleaned and separated shell halves into a steadily growing mountain on the foredeck, to be bagged later. Some days we would be packing shell until 9 pm, the last task being to sew up the hessian bags now stuffed with pearl shell and pile up the sacks like cordwood. When space ran out on the foredeck, the bags were piled wherever there was space.

After chopping and cleaning shell all day we would sail at night often for several hours to a shell dump marked with a radar buoy. This was where we stored our live shell until we returned to collect it before heading home to Broome. A radar buoy comprised a white foam float impaled with a large bamboo mast about three metres long, onto which was wired a tin reflector which could be detected by our radar. The float was connected by rope to a weight on the bottom next to the shell dump.

Sometimes floats got destroyed or torn off and lost, or strong currents dragged the weight away from the shell it was supposed to mark. There are many lost pearl shell dumps along the Eighty Mile Beach.

Before we reached the buoy we would have to empty the shell tank of live oysters, stacking the wire baskets along the side of the lugger. The tank was then scrubbed clean in readiness for the next day's catch. When we were up on the buoy Farley would yell for us to empty the baskets and all hands would quickly shake the shell loose, ensuring they fell in a tight pattern for easy collection at the end of the neap.

On several occasions when Farley really needed to offload some shell, we would head to the *Paspaley I* and get rid of some mother-of-pearl. This was an alternative form of torture, heaving up the dripping wet shell baskets onto the bigger boat, until all the live shell from the tank was loaded.

The weather was hot, but with the decks packed out with shell, I had to forgo my preferred sleeping spot and return to my bunk space below. It didn't help the healing of my lacerated hands and knees that our cheap foam mattresses tended to soak up the humidity and required constant drying. In the end, it was often so humid below deck that I went topside and threw my mattress across the stacked bags of shell, the cooling sea breeze outweighing any minor discomfort.

The Colonel dubbed the concentrated accumulation of wild pearl shell 'stuffer patches'. It was a good description. The sea bottom was stuffed with pearl shell, and we were all stuffed after hours of chopping, scrubbing and packing.

CHAPTER 5

The Japanese

It was on the return journey home from one of those neaps in early 1979 that tragedy struck the pearling fleet.

At nightfall, with the weather worsening, we noticed that one of the PPL luggers on our starboard bow was going about. A vicious sou'-westerly was blowing, and the sea was heavy for the time of year. Something had to be wrong. Then Farley heard the VHF distress call that a young Japanese diver called Tioshi had fallen overboard.

He was a relative of one of the Japanese veteran hardhat divers and someone I knew, though not well. Like the rest of us he used to drink at the Rocy. I remembered him with the other Japanese crewmen enjoying a beer before we set out for the neap.

Man overboard was not a common occurrence on the luggers; the biggest danger was for new arrivals still finding their sea legs. But this was a shocker of a night. I remember a hell of a din from the galley, where the pots and pans were clattering like a drunken percussion section under the stainless steel grille that prevented them flying around the room in rough conditions. Add to that the noise of coils of anchor chain slamming against the wooden sides of the chain locker, tools in the engine room bashing together, and the wooden joints in the masts creaking and groaning. The lugger was a very noisy boat in a storm.

Perhaps Tioshi was relieving himself over the side when he fell. It would not have taken much as luggers tended to roll, lurch and shudder as they punched into swells. Or he may have lost his inhibitions after a few drinks. That was the scuttlebut later, back in Broome. The Japanese crews often started celebrating the end of the neap as soon as their gear was packed away.

Abandoning our course, Farley turned the *DMcD* about and we joined the search being conducted under appalling conditions. The little lugger fleet was the only means of rescue for Tioshi. At the time, there were no sophisticated search and rescue facilities in Broome. No aircraft available at the other end of a radio call. A Royal Australian Navy patrol boat which might have been able to help was hours away off Rowley Shoals, unable to reach us because of battery problems.

I threw on a raincoat and climbed the ratlines straining to see the diver, but visibility was dismal. A relentless expanse of foam-whipped sea was all I saw. On board the *Paspaley I*, Akiri Wosomo and Chebastio, Papuan divers with excellent night vision, stood on the ship's bow peering into the night for hours, but to no avail.

We tried as best we could to coordinate a search pattern based on wind and tidal movement, but as the hours slipped away so did the prospect of rescuing Tioshi. We never found him.

His death at sea caused an angry outburst when the RAN's Attack Class patrol returned to Broome and its crew went on a ritual drunken bender at the Roey.

Feelings were running high and the prospect of an ugly brawl was barely averted by the intervention of cooler heads. It seemed incredible to us that the navy was unable to help. It was just another sad chapter in the story of the Japanese in Broome, a mixed story of connection and cooperation, suspicion and at times enmity.

* * *

IT IS impossible to tell the story of pearling and Broome without the Japanese. More than nine hundred headstones in the Japanese cemetery in Broome, not to mention numerous other lonely graves scattered around the Kimberley coast, are testimony to the courage of the Japanese divers, who used to be paid part of their fee before the season began because of the high risks of their work. Arthur Bligh, a white pearler at Broome at the turn of the twentieth century, donned the suit of one of his divers to try out the experience for himself, and later wrote about its solitary danger. The sea bottom was a 'Garden of Eden', he wrote, but the feeling of loneliness was 'dreadful', and hardly made up for the beauty:

There is no sound, everything is new and strange and much of the beauty is a snare for the unwary, as some animals and flowers have poisonous spikes or other protection which can hurt or kill you. In fact the power of protecting yourself from unseen enemies lessens on the sea floor and if there is danger about you are quickly in it.

Bligh was hauled up after a few minutes, bleeding from the nose and ears, and with other alarming symptoms. Depending on the skill of the tender – the deckhand who controlled his air and his entry and exit into the water – a diver could be fed too much or too little air, or pulled too quickly from the water, precipitating the bends. 'I saw many cases that had to have complicated treatment and many that left the sufferers helpless cripples,' Bligh wrote. 'In several further cases the divers were pulled up dead, crushed out of recognition. Their stomachs had been forced into their chest cavities, their faces were bloated, tongues black and swollen and eyes almost forced from their sockets.' Don McKenzie, longtime foreman of pearl graders at PPL's packing shed, vividly remembered witnessing a hard-hat diver brought ashore after an accident in which his air had been cut off. He was still alive, but his head was so swollen that his crewmates were unable to remove his brass hard-hat.

Many hard-hat divers died deep underwater in places with names like the Roebuck Deeps, near the modern Broome wharf, or the so-called Divers Graveyard in King Sound, off Derby. The Japanese would dive deeper than others, seemingly oblivious to the dangers of underwater

THE LAST PEARLING LUGGER

gutters and trenches and dangerous currents capable of tearing out an airline. 'It was dangerous if you went more than thirty fathoms (180 feet),' an old Aboriginal diver told me. 'In King Sound there were many deep holes. There was a lot of sickness there. You could see the pearl shell lying all over the place, but we Aboriginal divers floated over it. The Japs and Asians went down to the bottom.'

The original Japanese pearl divers came to Broome from the whaling village of Taiji in the prefecture of Hung Shui. By tradition, the men of Taiji hunted as a group, all putting to sea in long boats. One hundred of them died in a single incident when a whale rammed the boats. The story goes that it was a mother whale whose calf had been netted by the hunters. This terrible episode led to the collapse of the group hunting system, and as Japan began to open to the West, word spread of the pearling opportunities in northern Australia.

In the early days of Broome there were so many Japanese workers there that Chinatown was known as Japtown. By 1919 there was a population of about 1200 Japanese. They made up almost half the town's residents, and dominated the pearling workforce. Through the process of 'dummying', Japanese divers were able to buy their own luggers, and man them with all-Asian crew. The industry today is still shaped by their customs. Rice was always served at mealtimes on the luggers, and the first spoonful of rice was always tossed over the side, acknowledgement that if you took from the sea, you had to give something back. Pissing off the diving ladders was considered taboo on all boats, because of the Japanese superstition that it brought ill fortune. This prohibition was vigilantly enforced on the luggers, and is still observed on some of the new steel and fibreglass trawlers.

At the start of every season, the pearl fleet was assembled in Dampier Creek for the ceremonial blessing. A mangrove branch was cut and tied to the mast, to signify the safe return of crew to land. Then an old Japanese crewman would take a bottle of sake, and splash it liberally on the boat, particularly on the diving ladder, the main mast, the compressor and the engine. This blessing was followed by the lugger picnic, attended by friends and families as well as the crews. It was a major social occasion, celebrated with a feast of food and drinking – a 'gale force hangover' event according to Salty Dog, who first worked on the Broome luggers in the early seventies.

The years before World War I were good times, the 'Fat Years' when the pearling fleet was four hundred strong. But the outbreak of war and the invention of commercial plastics set the industry on its knees. Even though Broome was so remote from Europe, the conflict had a drastic impact on the pearling. Men left town to enlist, shell prices plummeted, and tonnes of shell remained unsold in warehouses and packing sheds along the Broome foreshore and Dampier Creek. The industry fell into a slump.

The community rebuilt in the twenties, and mother-of-pearl prices recovered, but the town had suffered, and continued to suffer, profound change. By 1939, only 73 luggers and 565 people were left working in pearling. The town was reeling from the effects of the Great Depression, misery compounded by a devastating 1935 cyclone, which struck the pearling fleet while it was at sea and caused 141 deaths.

THE LAST PEARLING LUGGER

Then war came again.

Japan's bombing of Pearl Harbor and the Imperial Army's rapid advance through southeast Asia changed everything. The local Japanese in Broome were rounded up. Some five hundred divers and crew, shopkeepers and cooks, many of them born in the community, were interned at camps as far away as Tatura in Victoria. Their wives were interned with them, even if they were not Japanese. Later, the pearling crews were transferred to POW camps because their intimate knowledge of Australia's northern waters was regarded as a security risk.

The lugger fleet was dismantled. Some vessels were commandeered by the military and later used in high-stealth resupply and rescue missions in Japanese-occupied Timor. The rest were loaded up and sailed south, or torched to prevent their being seized by the enemy in the event of a full-scale attack on Broome. Many locals by now feared they were in for it, and their apprehensions were not unwarranted.

Japanese warplanes raided Broome on 3 March 1942. With the fall of Java imminent, the small pearling port had suddenly assumed unforeseen importance. It had a sheltered harbour and an airfield suitable for heavy American bombers like the Flying Fortresses and B-24 Liberators. When the Japanese navy dispatched nine Zeroes to attack the town, it was crowded with American and Australian military personnel as well as military and civilian evacuees fleeing Java and other parts of the Dutch East Indies. Most of the local residents, particularly women and children, had been evacuated and Broome's pubs, school, and most of its private homes opened to the evacuees, but there were so many of them that large numbers remained on board the flying boats on which they had arrived, waiting for the next leg of the journey south to safety.

The Zero was a fearsome fighter equipped with cannon, machine guns and bombs. The Japanese planes swept down on the crowded flying boats in the harbour, strafing them without mercy. A Liberator plane with thirty-three sick and wounded servicemen aboard was blown in half and crashed into the bay. The raiders also attacked the RAAF base at Broome airfield, destroying every American, Dutch and Australian aircraft they found there.

When I was working on Farley's new boat, the *Roebuck Pearl*, we snagged the pick on one of these war wrecks – a Catalina – which had been lying on the sea floor out in the anchorage. Rather than inspect the wreck, which the powerful anchor winch dragged to the surface, Farley ordered us to 'get that fucking shit off my anchor' and, after much jimmying, back to the murky depths the old flying boat was consigned.

The Allies had anticipated trouble since Japanese reconnaissance aircraft had been spotted over Broome the previous afternoon. At 9.20 am the enemy planes swept in, leaving seventy people dead and twenty-four aircraft destroyed in their wake. At the same time, Wyndham was also attacked. Prime Minister John Curtin interpreted the raids as an ominous sign that the Japanese were considering capturing a port in the Kimberley as a base from which to attack the south.

Residents of Broome now believed the northwest was threatened by major invasion. The women and children, and many of the men, remained away until late 1943, as the raids continued intermittently for eighteen months. Businesses in Broome closed, and some never reopened. Some Japanese premises were looted and destroyed. Streeter's and Kennedy's stores were among those that remained operational for the duration. In August 1942, a bank manager who had been ordered to keep his branch open reported to head office that the population of the town then consisted of '65 whites, 30 aliens, 410 half-caste and 950 full-blood aborigines'. For weeks after the initial raid, civilians vacated the town every morning as a precaution. On 20 March, the airfield which was maintained by a corps of 180 indigenous and indentured workers was again attacked, with one casualty.

At the end of the war, the northern Australian pearling industry was moribund, but there were prospects of revival, if the fleet and the workforce could be rebuilt. In 1946, high quality pearl shell was commanding £500 a ton in New York. The post-war pearling boom lasted until 1957 when the plastics industry ensured pearl shell would become virtually worthless again.

The Australian government was predictably unenthusiastic about allowing the Japanese to return and reclaim their old pearling jobs, and there was local opposition in Broome. After two Japanese locals returned from internment in late 1946, Sam Male chaired a public meeting which heard objections from the Australian Workers' Union (AWU) and the Returned Servicemen's League (RSL). The RSL in particular strongly disapproved of the rehabilitation of the Japanese. Its president asked the meeting what legal right the people of Broome had to stop the Japanese coming back.

In response to such pressure, the Australian government sponsored a scheme to replace the Japanese divers with the famous sponge divers of Kalymnos. It paid for two crews to come out to work for pearling bosses; one went to Darwin, the other to Broome. The Broome experiment ended in tragedy when one of the divers died. The propeller of the lugger cut his air line, according to the coroner's report. Local gossips claimed that the accident would not have happened if Japanese were crewing the boat. The Greek divers found the local conditions arduous – the gear was different, older; the huge tides off Broome were dangerous; and the often cloudy waters contrasted with the clear, calm depths of the Mediterranean. Several of the recruits broke their contracts and went off to find work ashore.

The situation regarding Broome's Japanese was complicated. First of all, several of them were married to local women, who had bravely gone into detention with them. They had a claim to be part of the community, even if some whites didn't recognise it. Secondly, many of the pearling bosses wanted their Japanese workers to return, because they had so much of the industry's expertise. Once again the pearling masters used their political influence in Canberra. From 1953 Japanese divers and deckhands reappeared in official workforce figures, at first only in very small numbers. Many internees had been repatriated to Japan, but some brave Japanese returned to town. Kakio Matsumoto, a diver who had an Aboriginal wife, Helen Corpus, and four children, was one who came back.

Other Japanese with non-maritime interests also returned. The Shiosaki family came home intending to reopen their laundry business, only to find it was ruined. Then there was James Chi, the son of a Japanese mother and a Chinese pearler who had been a major identity in Broome's early industry. He considered he was probably safe from the round-up. Wrong. Chi was interned for four years, and shunned by whites when he came back to pick up where he had left off, running the local taxi service, marrying an Aboriginal woman, and raising his own family.

His son Jimmy became famous as one of the writers of *Bran Nue Dae*. When I lived at the Palace, Jimmy and other local musos would come and jam on our back verandah, and that's where I first heard a raw version of a song called 'Brand New Day'. For a while it was our dance anthem at the Roebuck Sunday sessions, every one shouting out the chorus: 'On the way to a brand new day, everybody, everybody say'. We all knew it was going to be a hit – though no one could have foreseen it would become an international hit musical.

But that's another story.

It was commercial pearl-farming that revived the flagging fortunes of the Australian pearling industry in the late fifties, and brought the Japanese back to northern Australia in numbers. Although William Saville-Kent, a Western Australian commissioner of fisheries, devised the principle of pearl cultivation in the late nineteenth century, Japanese technicians were first to patent a successful technique. By the 1930s there were hundreds of pearl farms in Japan. In particular, Kokichi Mikimoto's success in developing commercial pearl cultivation would be influential for pearling at Broome.

Given that the horrors of the Pacific war were still fresh in the minds of most Australians, and that there was continuing outrage at how Australian POWs had been treated by the Japanese Imperial Army, it would be a brave soul who formed a joint venture with Japanese pearlers. Yet when a delegation from Mikimoto's trading arm, the Nippo Pearling Company, arrived in the dowdy old port of Darwin in 1954, the visit created a stir. Its members made a lasting impression on Nicholas Paspaley's son, Nick junior, who was then a young boy: 'They were the first Japanese VIPs to come to Darwin. I remember the women were wearing kimonos. It was like receiving royalty.'

Two agreements involving the Japanese interests were signed, one for PPL to operate a lease on the Kimberley coast north of Broome, the other for Paspaley at Port Essington. First, there were a few hitches to overcome. The federal government under Robert Menzies banned Japanese nationals from owning 50 per cent of an Australian company, so the Japanese share was held in trust by the American firm of Otto Gerdau, which already was deeply involved in Australian pearling in its capacity as a buyer and seller of pearl shell. PPL's founders, Tokuichi Kuribayashi, Hiroshi Iwaki and Keith Dureau, called their pearl farm Kuri Bay, the name a homage to one of the Japanese principals. The lugger operations were supplied and managed by their Broome partner, Male and Co.

While the Port Essington venture initially failed to flourish, the Eighty Mile Beach fishery proved prolific, leading to the swift stockpiling of wild shell for cultivation. Kim Male, who studied accountancy by correspondence while working for the family firm, became a director of PPL. He remembers the Japanese staff arriving in an ex-tuna fishing boat with all their materials, camping on

Augustus Island until they finally established a permanent base at Kuri Bay. Heavy manual work such as the building of rafts, positioning of buoys and cleaning of shell was performed by contract labourers from Thursday Island.

Visiting teams of Japanese technicians would arrive at Kuri Bay to perform the seeding operation, a secret commercial process that was carefully guarded. This operation involves placing round beads of Mississippi mussel shell into a cut in the oyster's mantle, initiating the eighteen-month process by which layers of secreted nacre form to bind the artificial irritation that transforms into a cultured pearl.

Keith Dureau's son Dave, who was just a boy then, remembers an early visit to Kuri Bay, and the Thursday Island workers 'chairing' one of the Japanese guests ashore with all the pomp and ceremony normally accorded the royal family. It was little wonder that they were accorded special treatment. Broome in the 1960s was once more in the depths of financial depression. The commercial shell market had collapsed. Anyone not making a living from the supply of 'live shell' was out of business.

The Japanese controlled the local cultured pearl market, buying all the pearls produced at Kuri Bay. The profits flowed back to PPL allowing a steady expansion of the company. In 1964, PPL took delivery of a 38-metre steel mother ship, the *Kuri Pearl*, and a sister ship, the *Merinda Pearl*, three years later.

In 1976, Sam Male died, and Kim succeeded him as managing director of Male and Co, the third generation of his family to run a major pearling concern in Broome. It was in that part of the PPL business that the old traditions of Broome pearling continued to flourish, in the form of Streeters Jetty, the ancient packing shed at the top of it, and the old boatsheds located near Morgans Camp, a cluster of nondescript shanties tucked away out of sight, near the tidal mangrove belt lining Dampier Creek.

Only someone with no interest in the sea could resist the romance of the sheds. A first-time visitor was immediately struck by the marked aroma that hung in the air, a mix of the heady smells of pitch and oakum, a ropey material used by mariners since the Middle Ages to seal hull planks. There were usually at least a dozen men working away inside, indigenous shipwrights like Joe Roe and Doug D'Antoine, and Malays like Johnny Arum, who worked barechested, a tee-shirt wrapped around his head to mop sweat pouring from his brow. English was spoken as a second language, under a constant patter of Malay creole.

Kim Male set exacting standards for his fleet of luggers, which were put through a cycle of regular refits in these boatsheds. For many of the men who worked there, lugger maintenance was the only job they had known, skills often passed down from father to son. Their boss had grown up in Broome on the same unmade streets as his men. In his quiet way, he was passionate about Broome and its people, and in contrast to his grandfather he was known as a kind and generous man to work for.

By the time I arrived in Broome, PPL was Australia's oldest and biggest pearling enterprise. I hoped that at some stage I would work for the company: they not only paid the best money, but represented the true heart of the pearling industry. First of all, however, I had to find a way of becoming a diver.

CHAPTER 6

The twelve-tonne haul

Putting to sea from Broome, the Gantheaume Point lighthouse marked our last sight of town if we were sailing south. Then came Cape Villaret and Latouche Treville. All three landmarks had been named by the Frenchman Captain Nicolas Baudin on his voyage of exploration of this coast in 1801.

Next came Port Smith, Dick Morgan's base. It was followed by False Cape Bossut, our favourite mackerel ground, and much further south by Cape Bossut, with its solitary lighthouse.

Capes Frezier, Jaubert and Missiessy loomed in quick succession before the coastline became a seemingly endless series of glistening sand dunes. This was the start of the

Eighty Mile Beach, a bow-like arc of white sand stretching to Wallal Downs. On clear days you could see the station lying in a heat haze, the sun reflecting off galvanised water tanks. It was an eerie sight, stranded like a crashed UFO at the western extremity of the Great Sandy Desert. The submarine landscape was just as spooky, the water always tinged a sickly yellow-green, the bottom filled with snaky vegetation we called sea whips. My mate Wonder dubbed it 'The Lost World of Wallal'.

After our initial big strikes off the Three Sandhills, the *DMcD* began moving steadily south about six to eight nautical miles off the coast toward Wallal Station. At first we had the ground to ourselves because the four PPL luggers and the Gumboot, the nickname given to Paspaley's modified tuna boat, were fishing live shell rather than commercial shell. But after the PPL boats had met their quotas, several of their crew wanted to join in our bonanza and signed on as spare divers with Farley.

The heavy diving schedules took a physical toll on the divers, who were spending long hours in the water with only short breaks. Squire crunched the numbers and claimed that a day's diving was the equivalent of running for eight hours non-stop – almost equivalent to a marathon. On my first try-dive, I spent a half-day in the water and finished feeling physically ill and fatigued beyond speaking. This at a time when I had probably never been fitter in my life.

Commercial diving is all about working with as much comfort as possible, so that you can stay in the water for as long as possible, and return to it frequently. But comfort is a challenge when the pearl diver, festooned with neck bag, weight belt and breathing regulator, and tied by an umbilical air hose to the boat, is being dragged quickly along the sea floor by the moving lugger.

The divers' lips were torn and bruised by the constant pull of the regulator connected to 50 metres or more of air hose. The coarse neoprene wetsuits of the day were dubbed 'blue heelers' because of their 'bite' – painful chafing from hours of physical exertion under water. Every diver on the *DMcD* was afflicted, most commonly behind the knees, on the elbows, in the armpits and on the neck. At the end of one neap as he peeled off his wetsuit, the Colonel seemed to take on the appearance of a Tasmanian tiger, so numerous and severe were his rashes from this chafing.

The cockroaches which were a perennial problem on the luggers had a field day on Squire's wounds. 'My rashes were really hurting one night as I lay on my bunk. I reached over and felt a cockroach scurrying away from the bloody mess.' He became expert at detecting their feelers on the surface of his skin, and dashing them to the floor before they could bite.

The common preventive for wetsuit chafing was the liberal application of large dollops of Vaseline. What the supermarket girls back in Broome thought of the industrial purchases of the product by our crew is not recorded. We also tried nylon pantyhose with some success.

The condition had its funnier side. One celebrated break in Broome, after a prolonged drinking bout, Wonder Dog declared a painful condition known as 'Galloping Knob Rot'. When one of his women companions asked what he meant, Wonder Dog reached inside his jeans and in front of astonished pub patrons, including several tourists who had just decided to drop in for a quiet beer, he extracted his swollen red phallus swathed in plastic wrap, collateral damage from a new wetsuit.

On the boat, the divers would shovel down their breakfast and lunch as if they were making a pit stop to refuel, then jump straight back in for a 45-minute power drift. This had another painful side effect among the aquanauts – acute indigestion, or 'Freddy Feedback', as they dubbed it. The digestive process was under stress. 'Some of us were vomiting under water,' Squire recalled later. The cure of the day was an antacid compound called Mucaine, and divers would usually buy two large bottles to last them the neap. The Colonel lived off the stuff. It was such a vital diving aid we composed lyrics to celebrate its restorative power which we sang to the tune of J.J. Cale's 'Cocaine'.

There should have been a songbook of the Eighty Mile. The lyrics of Bob Dylan's 'Maggie's Farm' were changed to 'Ain't going to work on Farley's farm no more.' 'Hey Big Spender' was given a contemporary theme along the lines of 'The moment I came to the top – boom boom! I could tell it was a bend of distinction a real big bender. Hey big spender (Farley), bend a little joint for me.'

It was not just the work rate that was killing the divers' digestion. Often the unpleasant after-affects of dining on the *DMcD* were traced to Farley's distinctive à la carte menus, featuring dishes with names like napalm chook, spaghetti solitaire and his dreaded mackerel mornay. The latter usually came at the end of the neap when we had run low on other food and were reduced to eating the fish we had caught on the way down to the grounds. It was Farley's signature dish, pepper-caked chunks of mackerel floating in a pale muddy milk and cheese sauce of uncertain age and origin, with an optional side dish of rice. Divers gave it ten out of ten for reflux and ate it under duress, washed down with generous gulps of antacid.

When I was temporarily made O.C. of the kitchen in addition to my other duties as tender and deckhand, I thought I might indulge in a little scientific experimentation in the galley. My culinary efforts on my first trip out had been a disaster. Rice was a lunchtime tradition on the lugger, so I had emptied a bag of it into a pressure cooker, added what I thought was an appropriate amount of water, and turned up the heat while I resumed my work chopping shell.

After forty minutes one of the crew suggested that I should check on the stove because he thought he had caught a grain-based charcoal whiff emanating from below. I do not know what anti-alchemy had taken place, but I had successfully converted rice into concrete. Farley decried any food wastage, so I waited until he was busy then surreptitiously emptied the dense lump over the side. It disappeared with a resonating plop and went straight to the bottom quicker than a diver's lead weight.

That was not the end of the story. For several neaps after divers would come across a strange man-made mound on the sea bottom, shunned by all marine life – or so they said. Back in Broome, I urgently sought advice from a former girlfriend, music teacher Carol Sharp, who had recently arrived in town with one of my old schoolmates from Norwood High. She taught me the simple rule that the water must be about a knuckle higher than the rice to avoid culinary disaster.

Breakfast was always served after the first drift. With the divers burning huge amounts of energy it needed to be large, carbohydrate-rich and nutritious. Since the experts seemed to agree that indigestion was exacerbated by processed meat, instead of serving up the normal fare of scrambled eggs, toast, bacon and sausages I prepared a stewed compote of tomatoes and onions on toast. It was healthy and delicious, I thought.

Wrong. Drew was first to complain. 'Where's the bacon?' he asked, poking his fork into the tomato slurry in vain search of meat. 'There isn't any, it's a vegetarian breakfast,' I replied, trying not to sound like Pollyanna. He was not impressed.

Neither was Farley. 'It's a fucking fruit salad breakfast,' he snarled. There was a moment's pause before I shot back an equally caustic retort, courtesy of the J. Geils Band: 'Well if you don't like the breakfast, take out your false teeth and suck on your gums.' Farley responded by hurling a mug of hot tea over me before storming off to the stern of the boat. I was convinced my outburst would cost me my job.

He was already a bit shitty with me because I was the chief suspect in the disappearance of a packet of raisins he wanted to used for a scone mix (and truth be known, I had scoffed the lot). When we returned to Broome, I expected to be given my marching orders, but to Farley's credit he never again mentioned the incident. Mind you, I never served another vegetarian breakfast.

By now, word had got out about the shell-rich underwater acreages on which we were squatting, and the *Paspaley I* began to join us, more often than was to Farley's liking. When we discovered another 'stuffer patch', he was anxious to garner the lion's share for the

THE LAST PEARLING LUGGER

DMcD, and ordered an early start that morning to get a jump on our neighbour.

The sun's first rays were catching our boat when we weighed anchor and prepared to get underway. However, our early-morning manoeuvre had not gone unobserved by our neighbour. The venerable Nick senior was already up and in the wheelhouse of the Paspaley company flagship. Perhaps the sight of our lugger underway triggered some deep, instinctive competitive urge. Assuming his skipper had pulled the pick, the old man opened the throttle of the ship's mighty diesel power plant. Under full power from its 300-horsepower engine, all 125 tonnes of *Paspaley I* began to edge slowly and inexorably forward. But the ship's anchor was still firm on the bottom, and from the *DMcD* we watched in astonished silence as its heavy chain rose out of the water, stretching ever tighter.

It looked like the bow of the boat was being dragged under when the vessel suddenly listed and veered crazily to port as the anchor began to drag, in the process ripping an underwater trail of carnage through thousands of years of ancient biomass. This manoeuvre certainly served to shake the slumbering crew awake. After a few moments of undoubted panic, control was re-established on the bridge, the ship's engine put into reverse, and the anchor secured.

Most of the time, life on the *Paspaley I* was positively genteel in comparison with our lot. The shipboard attractions included scantily clad female deckhands recruited out of Broome. Not a few found a secondary role as comfort girls to the head diver Zimmo (Steve Zimmerle) and his pal, Sludge (Kevin Piper).

Bringing girlfriends on board could really test a relationship. A stunning beauty called Maggie arrived in Broome and fell into the amorous clutches of Dave Jackson, then a spare diver and deckhand for Paspaley. She was soon installed in Dave's suite at the Palace, and things went well until the fateful day when Dave suggested she come and work a neap on the boat. Halfway through the eight-day neap, Maggie changed bunks, taking up with Zimmo. Jackson was devastated and so was Zimmo – at his good fortune. But back on dry land, his Casanova appeal seemed to lose its gloss. One neap tide later the beautiful Maggie departed Broome as mysteriously as she had arrived, leaving a trail of broken hearts in her wake. She was last sighted in Bali.

Paspaley girls tended to be very attractive. They spent an inordinate amount of time sunning topless on the wheelhouse attired in nothing more than skimpy bikini bottoms like true sirens of the Eighty Mile.

While we were good friends with the Paspaley crew we reckoned they were spoiled rotten, with their unlimited hot water showers, ice-cream for dessert, airconditioned cabins and a leisurely work ethic which absolved divers from menial deck chores. This opinion found its most articulate voice in 'Shameless' Shane Ford, a veteran of the crayfishing industry, and the most recent addition to the *DMcD* crew to have once served on the *Paspaley I*. Shameless was passionate in the extreme. Whenever his former home and place of work sailed close by, it inevitably was made the target of a salvo of eggs. If there were no eggs to throw it was shell guts, potatoes, tomatoes – almost any food item lying about. The missile was normally accompanied by the war cry 'You're not on daddy's yacht any more', a reference to the luxurious conditions that our esteemed colleagues on the Gumboot enjoyed.

Despite our constant ragging of the Paspaley mob, to my recollection no *DMcD* crewman ever refused an opportunity for an evening visit and the chance to wallow under a hot shower, drink cold beer or scoff a bowl of frozen ice-cream. We would sit over our glasses, exchanging gossip and enjoying our proximity to the seductresses of the wheelhouse roof, looking forward to a chance to get to know them better when we all regrouped at the Roebuck Bay Hotel on the next spring tide.

* * *

THERE WERE still some great characters from the old pearling days working the waters off Broome. I think it was on my second neap in 1979 that Nicholas Mavromatis 'Mannie' Manolas hove into view. As the *DMcD* headed south to the Eighty Mile Beach and into open seas, we noticed an old scow rounding Gantheaume Point at the northern entrance to Broome port. It was the *Dawn*, a broad-beamed wooden barra boat that always reminded me of children's book illustrations of Noah's ark. Behind her on this occasion sailed a convoy of flimsy junks. It was a most unlikely scene, even to my unseasoned eyes. A gusty sou'easter was blowing, the sort that chops up the water and creates big swells. The floundering boats were full of Vietnamese refugees. Mannie, skipper of the *Dawn*, had found the boats as he motored down from Darwin, and was escorting them to the safety of Roebuck Bay.

He was a third-generation Greek–Australian seaman and a complete eccentric. His mother was Mary Dakas, the sister of Nick Paspaley senior, who on her husband's death was left several boats and a marine workshop down in Fremantle. Through hard work and good timing she was able to build up a fleet of pearling luggers. She started in 1949 with the *Swallow*, then Mannie built her the *Kestrel* on the beach at Broome, and the family was eventually able to add two more boats to the fleet. For almost a decade, her business prospered, but the pearl shell market's collapse in the late fifties ended her play. Unsaleable, the *Swallow* was left to rot in the sand.

Mannie had grown up in the company of people like his good friend Kim Male. He was twice skipper of a lugger, but he was also a natural rebel and maverick. The main thing he cared about was the sea. By the time I met him, he had a licence to fish barramundi in the estuaries of the Northern Territory. If ever there was a patron saint for all the rough-heads who served on luggers when I was a fisherman, it was he. Using only an echo sounder for navigation he sailed frequently between Darwin and Broome as routinely as most people would walk to the corner shop. The *Dawn* escaped the worst that Cyclone Tracy dished out in 1974 because Mannie, ever the canny old salt, sat out one of Australia's most devastating cyclones in the nearby Fennis River. Another time, he dropped into the Kuri Bay pearl farm with a blown head gasket. He amazed staff there by hand fashioning a substitute which he fitted himself before resuming his voyage.

He was an encyclopedia of information on old pearling grounds, able to reel off where we were likely to find patches of good shell bottom, and identifying nearby landmarks. Just as importantly, he remembered the dangerous or overfished locations to avoid. Speculation swirled around what Mannie was actually up to at sea, gossip which Mannie, with his wry humour, fostered with great enjoyment. In 1982 his boat sank in Roebuck Bay, the circumstances unexplained. When I asked him about it he swore to me that ASIO spies were responsible – as payback for help he gave East Timor after Indonesia invaded the former Portuguese colony in 1975. Many a punter drinking in the front bar of the Roey laughed and pooh-poohed the suggestion, reckoning that the ageing old *Dawn* had simply sprung a plank – or Mannie had. Nevertheless, those close to the old man insisted that he ran guns and aid to captive Timor, as well as rescuing Timorese refugees.

Almost as interesting in his own way was Dick Morgan, another son of pearling pioneers whom I got to know.

One fogbound September morning on the Eighty Mile, we'd been watching Dick Morgan's little concrete boat go about her business. The weather could close in suddenly along the Beach. A rolling bank of clammy fog would merge sea and sky into one, a hint of breeze and the gentle slap of calm water against the hull the only signs that we were moving, pushing across a great, grey infinite pond. Unable to sight the *Sea Venture* with the naked eye, we monitored her movement on the radar, noting the electronic blip of her regular and repetitive drift pattern. She was working about six nautical miles off Red Hill where an ancient pindan escarpment merges with the iron sands of the Pilbara.

Though we had cleaned up one shell patch and fished a very respectable tonnage we were attracted by Morgan's antics. So we set course for Red Hill and soon came up on the distinctive little boat as she emerged as a phantom apparition in the mist. There was nothing ghostly about the response of its owner when he saw Farley's black-hulled mariah bearing down. 'Go and find your own fucking patch,' Morgan yelled, as we set up for a drift.

We would soon discover the reason for his prickly response. The patch lay on a slight plateau that rose off a sandy bottom that was only 55 feet deep at high tide. Our divers jumped straight in and within a minute we heard the single long blast on the horn. They had found shell and Feeney immediately dropped a marker buoy so we could position the next drift over the patch.

'I have never seen so much shell. It was just loaded,' Squire told me later. 'After thirty minutes my work bag was stuffed full so I decided to surface and empty mine out before we turned round. I could see all the other divers feverishly trying to shake and pack in as much as they could.'

When the bags came up from the first drift we could hardly lift them over the side they were so heavy. We rigged a pulley block off the mizzen to help lift them out of the water. Squire's shell count was about 230, about the same for Droopy, while the Colonel and Big Bag each collected more than two hundred. It was a record drift with more than eight hundred pearl shells on board in less than sixty minutes.

By the end of the day more than 3500 shell were lying on deck, and over the next three days we fished a total of twelve and a half tonnes for the neap, a record for any pearl lugger. If it had been a marathon effort for the divers, the rest of the crew were totally overwhelmed by the mountain of pearl shell now piled all over the deck.

Farley began to worry that we were top-heavy, so we offloaded some bags of the cleaned pearl shell onto the *Paspaley I* to help stabilise the *DMcD* for our return to port. Yet, even lightened of more than twenty bags, the old lugger remained ominously low in the water, lower than we had ever seen her before.

Once the foredeck was stacked four bags high, we hauled the remaining bags across the stern where the wheel was located, laying them one on top of the other, leaving just enough space to steer the boat. When we could pack no more on the stern we tossed them into the galley, the engine room, across the narrow deck space separating the shell tank and engine room hatch, into Farley's cabin, jammed tight standing up along the gunwales, until we could not walk anywhere without tripping over bags of pearl shell.

We were fortunate that the sea was calm for the voyage home; nevertheless, the *DMcD* acquired a worrying roll from which she seemed to take an age to right herself. We reached Broome before sunrise and slept on board ready to dump the shell on the morning's high tide. At high tide we got underway, nudging the boat toward Town Beach. Attracted by the remarkable sight of a fully loaded pearling lugger, dozens of camera-wielding tourists from the nearby caravan park came down to watch.

Farley shouted the order, and dozens of bags of pearl shell splashed over the side. How strange to watch ten days of sweat and toil vanishing in minutes. If only it took the same time to collect the shell as to dispose of it. We ran the lugger back out to the anchorage and tidied up the boat. There was time for a quick counter lunch and a few beers before we would have to come down again and retrieve the bags at low tide. But first the shell meat had to be stripped from the rigging and emptied into several large plastic bins, cabins tidied, fridge emptied and swabbed out, and hatches secured, before we departed.

Little did we know it when we dumped our shell overboard that day, but the Colonel was about to jump ship.

CHAPTER 7

The cashed-up Colonel

The pearling bosses traditionally allowed their crews two free days on arrival back in port, unless turn-around time was short. There was always work to be done before the next neap: unloading the boats and packing shell; refuelling and watering; stores to be ordered and collected; hessian bags to be bought; fuel drums procured; a host of routine electrical repairs completed. In the case of the *DMcD*, the signal hose always required attention, along with the saltwater-prone solenoid which powered the anchor winch.

For crew lucky enough to work for PPL, much of this labour was performed by the port maintenance teams. When the luggers berthed at Streeters Jetty, the rickety little pier was transformed into a frenzy of activity and colour that to a first-time visitor might appear as a scene from another century. Time was always short, because the work had to be completed while the tide was in. The luggers carefully manoeuvred around each other in the narrow channel, queuing up for stores, fuel and water. In the sweltering heat Japanese and Malay crew, stripped to the waist, sweated and cursed as they heaved bags of commercial shell onto a rail trolley which was pushed a short distance along the track to the nearby PPL packing shed.

In the gloom of the old shed Aboriginal workers carefully graded the shell. Everyone knew their job, from the man who assembled the packing crates, to the shell sorters and the tally clerk keeping record in chalk on a slate board, all under the watchful eye of foreman Don McKenzie, who had been working at the shed since he was fifteen. There were eighteen grades of shell, from the top grades – O, closely followed by AAA, then AA, A, B, C and so on – down to R for rubbish. The graded lots were consigned to Otto Gerdau in New York.

Unlike the well resourced outfit at PPL, Farley's crew had to do our own shell-grading and packing. At low tide, we would collect the bags we had earlier tossed overboard. It was imperative that the work was done as soon as possible, because of the tendency of the shell bags to 'walk'. We tried to get down to the beach as soon as we could because the bags presented an attractive souvenir of their Broome holiday for tourists camped at the nearby caravan park.

All crew were required to take part, including the divers. Under the terms of our contracts we were classified as share fishermen. We shared the cost of fuel and food and the profits of pearl shell including any by-catch such as the dried shell meat.

We would drive down onto the beach in Farley's old four-wheel drive, towing a huge tandem trailer into which we loaded the shell. This usually took several trips. Back at Farley's yard we had a stockpile of fuel drums ready to be packed with shell. After the lids were cut out using a sharpened piece of car spring or a hatchet and mash hammer, the drums were cleaned with degreaser and readied for packing.

Shell was sorted according to its size and quality, then packed into the drums in much the same way you'd build a stone wall, flat and round shell hard against each other, a tedious job which we endeavoured to make interesting by competing to see who could pack the heaviest drum in the fastest time. Once the drum was filled, we replaced the lid and secured it in place by bashing two pieces of metal rod across the top to lock it in place. We then strapped them four to a pallet, and wrote the consignment note.

The whole process usually took a day, after which we were happy to take an advance off our wages and head down to the pub. But after we had finished packing the shell from the twelve-tonne trip, an argument erupted between Farley and the Colonel over working hours and conditions. For several neaps, the Colonel had expressed dissatisfaction with the amount of work the *DMcD* crew had to do while ashore compared with other lugger crew. He had expanded his catalogue of grievances to include complaints about the quality of food on board, particularly the lack of greens and other fresh vegetables. He had a point.

I could sympathise with the Colonel. We were doing a lot of unpaid extra work in tough conditions. In fact he pointed at my legs which were covered with festering sores and lesions as evidence we were working too hard. But if he expected support from the rest of the crew it was not forthcoming, for the simple reason that we were all making too much money.

Farley told the Colonel that if he didn't like the job he was welcome to leave. So he did, buying a six-metre aluminium boat and hatching a plan to go pearling in Exmouth Gulf. If he was upset about losing his position, he didn't show it. We would miss his daffy affability, but as Big Bag, who took over as head diver, pointed out to the rest of us, it would be a relief not to have to endure Jeff Wayne's musical version of *War of the Worlds* which the Colonel played with mind-numbing repetition whenever he was allowed near a cassette player.

*   *   *

SORTING SHELL guts is not a pleasant job, but it was a favourite pastime among the divers and deckhands of the *DMcD* because of the chance of coming across a natural pearl. I am not suggesting that Farley mistrusted his crew, but it is fair to say that he also took a close interest in the job. While the odds of opening a shell and discovering a gem pearl were long, the sheer quantity of pearl shell that we handled shortened them considerably. Occasionally we were rewarded by a lustrous gem or two gleaming among the great clumps of pearl shell gut sliding across the deck – including one beauty that slid under the scuppers and sank back into the deep.

THE LAST PEARLING LUGGER

Just as with gold nuggets, natural gem pearls excite feelings of jealousy as well as awe. Superstition suggests that they can bring bad luck to those who own or handle them; every one in the industry knows of cases where the lustre of a natural beauty has done strange things to people, driving a wedge between old friends and business partners, and irritating relations between crew and their pearling masters.

The *DMcD* was no exception. Its divers and deckies were contractors, not employees. The policy was that any pearls that were found would be surrendered to Farley: any profits from their sale would be shared or we could purchase the pearls back at a discount price. This undertaking seemed to work well until at some point in season '79 we noticed that the choicer gems we discovered were not being offered back. Rumblings of discontent quickly spread, in particular at Farley's partner, who had insisted on all crew signing into their contracts a hastily hand-scribbled amendment termed Appendix A, to the effect that all natural pearls remained the property of the company.

The effect on the crew who, up until that time had been scrupulously honest, was that if we were not to be trusted then we would respond in kind. It was against this background that the first whispers got around that a gem of extraordinary size had been found and kept by its discoverer. Rumour had it that while Farley was called away to attend to an air line, the Colonel had found a monster gem and quickly and surreptitiously slipped it into his Vaseline jar.

Personally, I thought that if the suggestion was true, then the Colonel was entitled to enjoy his good luck. I had not complained about my modest rate of six cents a shell, but ever since we had struck the stuffer shell patches I had quietly hoped Farley might offer a modest pay rise. Though he never made any secret of the fabulous wealth he was accruing from his mother-of-pearl sales, and openly boasted that it would fund the construction of a new trawler, the wage rise I hoped for was not forthcoming.

My sense of being exploited did not diminish until the day I slipped a pearl under my tongue, an act which by then felt entirely justified. If it was theft, so be it. What I took was not a small fortune in pearls, rather half a dozen low-quality gems discovered over the course of the season. Over ensuing seasons I learnt that I was a very minor offender compared with some other lugger crew. The practice was widespread.

Soon, the old team was breaking up, much to my regret. It was not only the Colonel who wanted out. At the end of the season, on the *DMcD*'s last trip home from the grounds, Big Bag and Squire broke the news that they intended to go their own way. They had agreed to buy the old lugger from Farley, then acquire a southern fishing licence out of Onslow and start their own pearl farm.

There was no big break-up party at the end of the season. We collected our last cheques from Farley and went our separate ways. Big Bag and Squire's caravan set off down south to Onslow and their new venture. I was sorry to see them go, but it was not as if they were shorthanded. There was plenty of volunteers eager to work for them, and I had taken too much of a liking to Broome to move south.

There was something about the place – the sheer diversity of life there, the town's history, and the pervading influences of Asia – that much attracted me. There was nothing to match Friday nights at the Roebuck, an evening in the open-air Sun Picture Theatre, or warm nights with a friend under the stars at Cable Beach.

So I declined Big Bag's offer of deck work, pinning my hopes on a Broome-based diving job. For that I needed to get some experience and underwater hours logged. Mark Walsh, a diver for Dick Morgan, had taken a berth with Steve and Bruce, and he gave me the idea that maybe Morgan would need a try-diver. If all else failed, I figured that I could probably rejoin Farley, who was hiring crew for his new boat, the *Roebuck Pearl*. We had our differences, but I respected Farley. In the meantime, in a few weeks I would head back to Melbourne to see my family for Christmas, then purchase a four-wheel drive with my earnings and return to Broome.

My mate Wonder Dog had decided to head straight back to his family down south. As I sat in my room in the Palace, studying the progress of the bougainvillea snaking its way around my room, I heard in the distance the turbo-charged roar of the Gascoyne Traders road train beginning its long haul down to Perth, 2400 kilometres away. When it passed my window, I heard the unmistakeable voice of a passenger, Wonder Dog screaming into the wind: 'You can all get fuuuuuucked.'

Other crew decided to work through the long humid summer. Mark Feeney and Shameless Shane could never get enough of fishing boats and salt air and ducked down south to work the crayfish season. Russell Massey stayed on to do freelance work after a start-up venture was announced by Broome Pearls. Its principals, John Foxlow and Ian Turner, had the backing of Perth-based fishing tycoon M. G. Kailis, who provided a short-term loan of a modified Gulf trawler to fish the Eighty Mile. Along with Farley's acquisition of the *Roebuck Pearl*, this was an important development in the industry.

The new generation of pearl farmers needed bigger, more modern boats. As the Fisheries Department licensed bigger pearl shell quotas, pearling masters required new vessels. They had to have a larger cargo capacity for commercial mother-of-pearl catches, more spacious accommodation and bigger cold stores in order to stay on the grounds longer.

The days of the working pearling lugger fleets were drawing to a close. It was nearly the end of their era. They had been wonderful workhorses of the sea, but were costly to maintain and increasingly limited in their capacity to operate efficiently in a period of rapid modernisation. The new breed of pearl farmer like Farley needed big steel or fibreglass converted fishing trawlers. Only smaller operators like Steve and Big Bag, in the process of establishing their venture, could make do with the lugger because their shell quota was more modest.

* * *

THERE WAS a postscript to the '79 season, concerning the Colonel. For a while after he went his own way, our old crewmate had seemed happy to enjoy a more relaxed lifestyle with his girlfriend, spinning his wheels in his new boat off Riddell Beach near the port of Broome. It was there while he was perfecting a series of high speed manoeuvres that he achieved what he had narrowly avoided in the lugger, running aground. By all accounts it was a surreal incident. Witnesses agree that apart from the cowboy hats they wore, the Colonel and his girlfriend were as naked as the day they were born. As Big Bag told it later, he caught a glimpse of 'a pair of sunburnt arses', the Colonel with one arm round his girl and the other on the helm, moments before they struck the reef.

True to form, John emerged unscratched and unfazed. Repairs were made and he set off south on his pearling trip in Exmouth Gulf. Some months later, he bumped into Big Bag, Squire and Feeney in Onslow. At some point (probably over drinks), the Colonel revealed he was the owner of a whopping sixteen-millimetre natural pearl – more than half an inch in the old measure – and was keen to contact a pearl trader for a sale.

Just how he had acquired the pearl was unclear. Some members of the *DMcD* were under the impression that he had found it while he was working on the lugger, but the Colonel said he had found it in Exmouth Gulf. Regardless, it was sold for a handsome sum, about $20,000, to a UK-based pearl shell dealer Hamburger and Son. Hamburger in turn sold the pearl to Arab interests, and I believe it was later X-rayed and found to be two pearls fused together. A jeweller separated the pair and the pearls were resold as a package, for a small fortune.

Meanwhile Farley picked up wind of the deal and blew a gasket, pressing charges of theft against the Colonel. Relations between the two seemed to have been permanently impaired by the Colonel's criticism that his old skipper acted like a slavedriver. A trial was held in 1980, and several former crew were called as witnesses, but the Colonel stuck to his version that he had found the pearl in Exmouth Gulf, and the case was dropped for lack of evidence.

Perhaps Farley was able to console himself with his new pearling venture. His much vaunted steel trawler was under construction in Lombardo's shipyard at Fremantle, and with the proceeds of the 1979 season, his company Roebuck Deep Pearls was off to a flying start.

Farley was a hard-arse when it came to money. Feeney, who used to live near him in Broome, told the story of how one evening he and Big Bag had heard a frightful din coming from the skipper's house. Sneaking across the road, they took cover behind some bushes and watched Farley in heated negotiations with Jack Krasenstein, a mother-of-pearl dealer from Perth. At one point the argument became so ridiculously heated that Feeney and Big Bag feared their hiding place would be discovered – they were laughing so loudly. But the seller and the buyer were so embroiled in details that they didn't hear a thing.

CHAPTER 8

Diving in

The weather was changing. It was late November and the hot, humid build-up to the wet season had begun. The cooling monsoon rains would not begin falling until December, so I had to content myself with watching spectacular displays of forked lightning ripping across the night sky.

Before I left Broome that summer, our landlord at Bishop's Palace dropped a bombshell. He had decided to demolish the grand old building in order to build a block of brick flats. Its long-term residents were stunned, but there was not so much as a whimper of opposition from Town Hall, save for the lone voice of former diver turned shire councillor Dave Dureau.

I had been helping out at the *Broome News* whenever I was in town. We began a media campaign to raise support for the Palace's preservation. Cheap accommodation was as hard as ever to find in Broome, particularly for pearling workers. Unless you were employed by PPL and accommodated in their single men's quarters, the options were very limited in the off-season. The destruction of the Palace would create even greater hardship, but our campaign was about more than this: it was about a distinctive building and the oddball community life that went on there, free and easy, eccentric and seedy. Palace society would never be replicated in the two-storey brick block of units that would replace it. For the first time, I think I understood that Broome was not going to remain the completely magical place that it had been when I found it.

Our case was publicised by the ABC's Bill Peach, who interviewed me outside the historic residence. It was a faltering, emotional performance on my part. Inevitably, our resistance proved futile. One morning the front end loader arrived and that was the end of our happy Palace lifestyle. This act of destruction put a dampener on things and I was glad to get away to Melbourne to spend some time with family and friends.

I was cashed up and proud of my savings, but I was also a subscriber to Timothy Leary's hydrodynamic theory of money – when you have it, spend it like water. I decided to buy a decent four-wheel drive. Among the many car yards along the Maroondah highway in suburban Ringwood, I found a recently traded, late-model Land Cruiser with tray, a solid workhorse well suited to life in the rugged northwest. The price was about $8000 and I paid cash, a memorable experience.

I combined a test drive with a camping expedition with friends bush bashing along old forestry trails that criss-crossed deserted gold diggings in the rugged Victorian Alps. One night as we sat relaxing around the camp fire, the younger brother of an old schoolmate used a disparaging term – 'coon' or 'gin jockey'. I took the comment personally partly, I guess, because at the time I was smitten with Eunice Yu, younger sister of Peter Yu, chairman of the Kimberley Land Council. I had first met Eunice at the Roey, where she used to hang back a bit from the rest of the crowd. She was shy and smart, and would soon figure out that commitment was not my middle name, not at this stage of my life anyway. We ended up good friends.

In no uncertain terms, I told my mate's younger brother that his comments were uninformed and wrong. We spoke about my experiences in Broome and the Kimberley generally, of a culture that had been caught in the ways of the white man and trapped unhappily in enforced detribalisation. I acknowledged there were widespread problems with grog, but argued that it was not unique to the indigenous community, just more visible. It was a tense exchange. I could hear The Police's 'Message in a Bottle' thumping away repetitiously on a cassette player in the background, and I kept thinking how ironic that was.

Given that the Palace had been reduced to a pile of broken boards and mangled corrugated iron, I needed to sort out my future accommodation, and a caravan seemed like the best short-term option. So I decided to drive to Broome, stopping in Perth to purchase a caravan, then towing it north. It would not only be a welcome chance to see more of the country. I had been invited to the wedding of an old school mate, David Harris, yet another of my friends who had tried life in Broome for a while, but had eventually gone south to a job in radio in Perth.

Norm House, the mate who had put me and Al up when we were passing through Alice Springs, was back in Melbourne. He seemed to have caught the Broome bug, and decided to come along for the journey. My invitation said 'Mark and Friend', so I RSVPed that I would attend and bring a friend as suggested.

Our plan was to hit the Nullarbor Plain via a short detour through the famed wine growing regions of the Barossa and Clare valleys of South Australia. Before we hit the road we bought a stash of green flake, optimistically imagining that the ounce in the glove box would last us to Broome, balance to be shared with friends on arrival.

Looking back, I have to admit that this was a stoned transit of the continent. There was one bizarre sunrise stop outside a winery in the Clare. We had already smoked our first joint – it must have been 6 am at least – before we rolled up the driveway, looking forward to a morning tipple before hitting the road again.

The owner looked like he had just got out of bed, the reason perhaps that he seemed less than keen to facilitate an early morning tasting after we had signalled our arrival with a social blast on the car horn. Muttering something about opening hours he grudgingly unlocked his grog shop, and eyeing us with a malevolent stare he shoved us the wine list saying: 'S'pose you want to start at the top and work down?' He could recognise a couple of wine connoisseurs when he saw them. Hours later, we poured ourselves out of the winery, having been temporarily delayed by the flirtatious advances of his daughter.

In Perth, I purchased a caravan for the bargain price of $1200. We reached Port Hedland just in time to catch the tail of a cyclone. Normally dry and arid, the surrounding countryside was a blanket of green; as we approached the De Grey River much of the flat desert country was actually submerged. About sixty kilometres north of the iron ore town, the river was in flood and the bridge impassable. The ramp leading onto the causeway had washed away. We set up camp on the southern side along with the rest of the traffic headed north, waiting for the floodwaters to subside.

Among the great clumps of debris caught in the turbocharged caramel deluge that day I saw virtually every species of snake that I could name. Eventually we got underway again, the blacktop soon turning to familiar red pindan dirt on the unsealed last leg of highway which leads to the Broome turn-off. From there it was just a short hop to the welcome sanctuary of the Roebuck's front bar.

We were in good company. It was late January and other pearling crew were beginning to arrive in town. Wonder Dog was due to start a full-time contract with Allan Badger on the lugger B-3. Intent on solving his accommodation problems, before he left Perth he had purchased a caravan and hired a truck driver to tow it to Broome. He had been looking forward to moving into this new home. But the caravan's brakes seized just out of Port Hedland, and the resulting friction started a fire. Within minutes the van was a blazing pile of plastic on the side of the highway, with all Wonder's belongings inside it. The truckie's short-lived attempt to extinguish the blaze was not helped by the presence of a large stash of .303 rounds in the van, which quickly started cooking off in the heat blasting through the walls. By all accounts the incident resembled a scene from *Mad Max 2*.

Despite his caravan tragedy, Wayne arrived back in town in style, in a BMW coupe driven by younger brother Larry (Junior Dog). A new face, Kim Harvey, a friend of Wonder Dog's and former cray fisherman, came up from Perth with his mate Dave Baldock. Shameless Shane was also there with Pam, the woman who had the rare privilege to call herself his girlfriend. After a less than successful attempt to convert Pam's late model Corolla into a cabriolet by removing the roof with an angle grinder (on a visit to Perth, she was unaware of the modification), the couple thought it time to leave crayfishing and make a fresh start at reconciliation. They had decided to move up from Leeman and base themselves permanently in Broome. Paspaley's 'white divers', Steve Zimmerle and Kevin Piper, drove in, the former arriving from Queensland in a shiny new, fire-engine red Toyota four-wheel drive.

Wonder managed to secure a billet in PPL's colonial-era single men's quarters in Chinatown. Harvey, better known as Kimberley Cool, was looking for work and hoping to get a start with newcomer Broome Pearls. At first, he stayed in the PPL quarters, but after a week or so he was sprung as a squatter and ordered out to join the rest of the serfs at the Bali Hai. He and Baldock shared a two-man nylon hiking tent – until it burnt down during a drunken party several weeks later.

THE LAST PEARLING LUGGER

Norm and I had also pitched camp at the Bali Hai caravan park, just as Al and I had done the first time I came to Broome. Norm set up a huge canvas cottage tent next to my caravan. He scrounged some pallets and carpet and it quickly took on a homely appearance, serving as a frontier command post for itinerant pearlers looking for a party or a crash pad for the night.

I had never lived in a caravan park before and this one had some real personalities. There was a middle-aged divorcee who virtually lived at the naked beach and when she wasn't there would make social calls on us for a cold beer in a state of near undress. Not that we were strangers to the nudist zone ourselves. A dark tan was the best evidence of our northwest credentials. When we weren't out looking for work we would head down to the beach and lie under the baking sun for hours on end, in between ocean dips that might involve a short stroll of just a few metres or a kilometre's hike, depending on whether the tide was in or out.

Most evenings were spent with friends in the front bar of the Roebuck or the back bar of the Continental with its juke box which always seemed to be playing the Boom Town Rats' 'I Don't Like Mondays', the big hit of that summer. But money by this time was getting a little tight for us both. I had not received an invitation from Farley to work another season with him. Nevertheless, several of my ex-crewmates had called to say the job of deckie/spare diver was there if I wanted it. Farley and I had parted company on good terms and divers and deckies who had worked a full season or near enough on the legendary *DMcD* the previous season appeared to have little trouble getting work. In a way, a second season with Farley was tempting, but I still wanted a shot at direct-entry diving, even though I had no experience save for the brief paddle around the lugger a few months earlier.

Norm had marketable skills and wasted no time in finding a job. He was an experienced barman, bouncer, truck driver, plant operator, and mechanic and if he got desperate there was always art, perhaps a quick impressionist rendering of our campsite. Within days of arriving in Broome he had proved his street credentials. It happened at a wild party at the Broome Pearls house at the top of Guy Street, when he punched out a drunken ringer from Waterbank station who had been bothering some local Broome women.

He began work for a colourful local contractor, Ted Foster, a self-made businessman and hardened nor'-wester with a build like a beer keg. Ted owned a Mack water tanker which was working outside Broome on a big road project to seal the last stretch of dirt on the northern highway. He had been looking for a driver for weeks and I'd given up trying to convince him my Victorian articulated licence entitled me to pull something bigger than a caravan. After proving his mechanical credentials by making repairs to Ted's truck, Norm was rewarded with the driving job and set off within days for a remote bush camp.

Soon after, he was back in town having managed to get work with Broome Pearls, Ian Turner and John Foxlow's new venture. He ended up working alongside a volatile Vietnam veteran named Wes, driving the company's Shark Cat down to the Eighty Mile, running supplies to the *Pacific Lady* and collecting the live shell its crew had collected, which was then dumped at Broome Pearls' lease in Roebuck Bay. Wes was a former commando; Turner, the boss, was an anti-war activist who went to jail for resisting conscription during the Vietnam War. Norm had to physically separate the pair during some angry exchanges in which Ian faced getting the worst of it.

Other vacancies in new pearling ventures began to open up, apparently inspired by Farley's successful assault on the big operators' hold on the industry. Dr Peter Reid, Broome's community medico, acquired a pearling lease off Willy Creek north of Broome. Shameless, Pam, and my old pal Al Burton were hired to build the camp and dive for pearl shell using a Shark Cat even smaller than the Broome Pearls boat.

Shameless's notoriety as the wild man of Western Australia's crayfishing industry was well established by the time he arrived in Broome. Needless to say, there were some legendary parties at Willy Creek. But as we had already discovered when he worked on the *DMcD*, Shane's other talents as a diver, deckhand and general master of improvisation, made him an invaluable employee.

Reid's operation was a shoestring venture and suffered for it. It wasn't long before his other partners, Shire President Des Haynes and local identity Dave Ray, began to have second thoughts about the viability of the enterprise. Despite grumbling about costs the company persevered. The owners paid a visit one day, Doc Reid equipped with a six-pack of beer and his medical bag, as he prepared to investigate the anatomical mysteries of the pearl shell.

There were frequent mechanical breakdowns on the Shark Cat, and parts had to be air freighted up from Perth, with more delays and more expense. During down time, fishing for barramundi and salmon was popular. So was stalking mud crab which lived along the creek's mangrove-infested inlets. Shameless would go beachcombing along the coast and over several weeks his wanderings yielded a treasure trove of Aboriginal artefacts, shards of pottery and ancient grinding stones.

To supplement their meagre earnings, Al and Shane used the farm's bush bomb, a heavily modified Land Cruiser, to tow stranded tourists and their four wheel-drives when they became stuck in the treacherous tidal mud flats around Willy Creek. On reflection, this enterprise probably earnt them more money than pearl diving.

I managed some short-term contact work as a chain man with Bill Hart, a Derby-based surveyor and direct descendant of the Harts who produced Steve Hart of the Kelly gang. Bill needed a chain man to help with a survey of the Aboriginal communities along the Dampier Peninsula north of Broome, land which was to be formally recognised as native title. We agreed on a daily rate and off we set in Bill's battered old red ute, churning up a huge red dust cloud in our wake as we charged up the Cape Leveque track.

It was exhausting dragging a metal tape (a chain, as it is known) through coastal scrub while Bill took his measurements on his theodolite and banged in survey pegs. Yet the work was also fascinating. It took us to Beagle Bay, a former Catholic mission on the western side of the peninsula, with a historic little church which had been built by local people under the supervision of German Pallottine priests during World War I. Its altar was inlaid with gleaming pearl shell collected from the beaches, its ceiling with other shells representing stars. The job gave me a deeper understanding of the contacts between the pearling industry and indigenous language groups living around Broome. With the permission of local elders, we traversed culturally sensitive areas still used for initiation.

Bill took pride in being an old-school surveyor; he shunned the new laser theodolite technology. He was immensely practical, planning to complete a boundary survey for a Kimberley cattle station by working at night taking star shots. It would be cooler, he said. We remained good friends and after my return to pearling work I would often drive up to Derby to visit.

* * *

THE CASH I earnt surveying tided me over until, as I had hoped, a friend recommended me for a diving job with Dick Morgan at his pearl farm at Port Smith. Morgan had a reputation for low pay and long hours, but it was a valuable opportunity to secure the diving experience I needed if I wanted to work for PPL.

The Morgan family's involvement in pearling dated back to 1919 when Dick's father, Alf, returned from World War I and was hired as a pearl shell opener by the firm of Streeter and Male. In 1971 (the year Alf died) the family moved to Port Smith from their first pearl farm in Exmouth Gulf. The site seemed idyllic enough, an enchanting tidal inlet 250 kilometres south of Broome, between False Cape Bossut and Latouche Treville. But it was ravaged by cyclones and also by a devastating pearl oyster disease which eventually wiped out 80 per cent of the shell stock. This was a cruel blow to a hardy family of pearling pioneers who at enormous personal and financial cost had carved out a working operation from this remote bush location, including a homestead with full amenities and a small airstrip for Dick's single-engine Cessna 172.

By the time I arrived on the scene, Dick was packing up, preparing to abandon the lease at Port Smith and move south to Exmouth. The final straw had been the cyclone that Norm and I had encountered at the De Grey River. It had slammed across his pearl farm, burying thousands of shell, and he needed a diving team to salvage whatever shell he could find after the disaster, including thousands of dead shell which could still be sold for a good price as mother-of-pearl.

I didn't know it when I started, but the Morgan family was really struggling and had been forced to sell property in Perth to compensate for the huge setback at Port Smith. This helped explain Dick's attitude. At the time, I just assumed he was mean. He asked if I could find some empty fuel drums and bring them down to Port Smith when I came. I located some at a local fuel depot and loaded them on the back of my truck, roping them down for the drive south. But Morgan offered no thanks when I dropped them off, just a gripe that had he loaded the drums he could have stacked about twice as many.

Before I began work I also had to procure some diving gear. I didn't have enough cash for a new wetsuit so foolishly, in retrospect, I bought a second-hand set of long johns from the Colonel and an ill-fitting top from another friend. It was a thick, heavy suit that left me with festering welts and bloody chaffing after hours spent underwater.

The one item I had to buy new was my regulator or demand valve, a vital bit of kit that enables divers to breath. It consists of mouthpiece, diaphragm, valve and a length of air hose with a snap connector. I also bought a brand new face mask. These are highly individual items for divers and my selection was a black low-volume mask with the glass set close to my face. I preferred the softer blue fins to the hard black type preferred by some of my diving mates. A weight belt (with three weights) and booties completed my equipment fit-out.

I was billeted in a comfortable crew quarters, accommodation for his predominantly Malay and Vietnamese work force. Dick was very much in the mould of an old master pearler. Dinner was an anachronistic ritual, or so I thought: coloureds and Asiatics were fed on deck, whitefellas sat at the captain's table. Years later it occurred to me that this may have been the preference of the Malays themselves.

I spent the first few days helping pack shell and generally tidying up around the farm. Morgan needed a couple more deckhands so I told him of my friends Kim Harvey and Dave Baldock, who I thought would be keen for the work. Morgan agreed to hire them. I would drive back to town to find them, then Morgan would fly to Broome and collect us all. It was a long straight road back north cutting across the vast Roebuck Plains, an ancient river delta formed millions of years ago. As the red soil pindan plain flashed past I was at peace with the world, left arm on the wheel, right arm resting on the window and a tape of Brit ska rockers The Specials thumping out a reggae beat.

In Broome, Harvey was busy on something else, but I rounded up Dave and another mate, Shane Roberts, and we flew back with Morgan after first signing on with the fisheries department. I was surprised how easy it was to get a pearl diver's licence from the Western Australian Fisheries even though I had such limited diving experience. In 1980 the relationship between the fisheries department and the pearling companies was still very chummy.

Back at Port Smith, when we put to sea in the *Sea Venture*, I found that the purpose-built ferro-cement trawler, though smaller than the luggers, was actually a more functional work boat. The craft was in tip-top condition and a credit to its owner.

Our initial job was to try and recover dumped pearl shell now covered by sand thrown up by turbulence during the recent storms. As a novice diver, I was thankful we were starting in relatively shallow water about eight fathoms (48 feet) at low tide. We began work at dawn before the day heated up to temperatures around forty degrees. Dick soon located the general area of the first dump by dead reckoning, the radar buoy marking the location having long since blown away.

The engine-powered compressor was cranked into operation. To prepare for the dive, I rubbed a generous dollop of Vaseline under my armpits and the backs of my knees to help prevent chafing. Then it was on with the wetsuit, flippers and weight belt. I also rubbed a thin film of toothpaste inside my face mask to prevent it from fogging, and then blasted it clean with the deck hose.

THE LAST PEARLING LUGGER

It smelt quite antiseptic and pleasant, much better than soy sauce used by the Japanese for the same purpose.

I grabbed my neck bag and one of the Vietnamese tenders passed me a work bag which I clipped onto the down-line. Then I gave the regulator a quick purge to check air was flowing before stepping off the diving ladder into the deep blue sea. My first sensation was how good it felt to be floating serenely downwards, finally off the rocking boat. My ears cleared and I was able to equalise by swallowing. Now I was entering a silent world, with no noise save for a reassuring tump, tump, tump from the compressor.

Visibility was not particularly good, only about five metres. In the distance I could see the hazy outline of Sabri, the Malaysian head diver. He was already looking for shell, his flippers kicking up a thick cloud of sediment. The sea bottom off Port Smith was not an idyllic underwater paradise of tropical fish, multi-hued coral and giant clams. The cyclone had left it dull and monotonous, banks of sand interspersed with large strands of tawny coloured sponge-like plants waving in the current.

Occasionally I would drift over a cylindrical hole like a well made of small stones. Its sole occupant was a fish with large bulbous eyes like mine after a bad hangover, which spent most of its daylight hours standing on its tail. We called this species Monkey fish. As we approached their nests they would scuttle back into their holes, peering up at us with huge frightened eyes as if we were some sort of sea monster. When we had passed, up they popped, eyeing us carefully to ensure we were really on our way.

In those early weeks, diving all day physically drained me. As my body became used to hours of immersion in salt water I began to notice other subtle changes. My nasal passages began to discharge a mucous substance after hours of having compressed air pumped into my lungs.

Frequent ascents to bring up full work bags packed with dump shell collected from the mess scattered across the bottom brought on a feeling of slight giddiness at the end of my fourth day. It eased when I was back in the water but, on the fifth day just after dinner, one of my knees began aching intensely. A bend, or bubble of nitrogen, had lodged in my joint, a result of too many fast ascents even though the water was only about eight fathoms.

For every eleven metres dived in ocean water, nitrogen pressure inside the body increases. The deeper one goes, the more the nitrogen builds up, dissipating at a much slower rate than the carbon dioxide we breathe out of our bodies. The effects can be understood by thinking about a can of soft drink. If you open it gently, the carbon dioxide inside it rises to the surface with a slight fizz; but if you shake the can violently before you open it, there is an explosion of foam as the bubbles are released. Similarly, for the diver, too rapid an ascent causes nitrogen to emerge from tissue as bubbles and lodge in the joints.

Bad cases produce decompression sickness, with awful symptoms including itching, swollen lymph nodes, rashes and giddiness, tingling skin and blurred vision. Depending on the severity of the condition, treatment varies from re-immersion and a carefully staged ascent, to a visit to a hyperbaric chamber for recompression, in severe cases. In 1980, the nearest chamber was 2400 kilometres away in

THE LAST PEARLING LUGGER

Perth. This knowledge worried me slightly. The pain in my right knee lasted a couple of days and eventually disappeared, but it served as a warning to dive with more care.

With most of the pearl shell collected and packed, Morgan was ready to leave Port Smith, closing a chapter of northwest pearling. He had built a very beautiful home and substantial outbuildings, and the place was testimony to his resourcefulness, practicality and can-do frontier attitude. Pearling was such a tough game that hardship was a common denominator for solo operators like Morgan, and he seemed resigned to the turn of events. What he actually felt about it, he never let on.

He flew us back to Broome in his Cessna, a journey unremarkable except for my attempt to get some aerial shots as we approached the town high above the tidal mud flats, bounded by a turquoise sea. I flipped open the side window to poke out my Nikon camera, and nearly lost my arm in the slipstream as a jet blast of cold air streamed into the cockpit while Morgan prepared to land the aircraft.

I had logged valuable diving hours which would serve me well in a search for a better paid job. My wait would not be long. For now, though, it was back to the Roey.

CHAPTER 9

The Roey

You had to love the Roebuck Bay Hotel. News of the fleet's impending arrival in Broome was never more warmly welcomed than there. The amply proportioned manager, Terry Cullen, better known to us all as Top Cat or TC, would roster on additional barmaids just to cater for the two-day drinking spree that normally followed our landing on the spring tide.

A former wrestler and Vietnam vet, TC was a huge man in equal measures of girth and mirth. Nevertheless, he had a deadly and effective way of handling troublemakers. Over-imbibers inclined to a bit of biffo faced his immediate wrath if they were foolish enough to ignore a first and only warning.

He would emerge like the Incredible Hulk from his back office as barmaids pointed out the offenders. His eyes would narrow to two black slits, his expression became ominous and menacing. Striding forth purposefully toward those miscreants who dared disturb the peace, he would secure the pathetic cretins in a crushing neck lock under his massive trunk-like arms. Depending on his mood, they might be evacuated at the trot through the bar's batwing doors, their skulls pile-driven into the nearest verandah post. Justice north of the twenty-sixth parallel was harsh but effective.

Whenever TC was busy taking care of hotel business in the back room, security was delegated to two bouncers. The amiable Carl Sputore, still in his mid-twenties, stood about six feet two inches and was blessed with film-star good looks and an athletic body that was coveted by a legion of women admirers. He was more than happy to accommodate their admiration, as his nickname Italian Stallion suggests. His counterpart, Dave McKewen, was not much older and a different type altogether: a gruff, hard-drinking former debt collector and one-time police officer.

Over consecutive springs, this pair became our allies, friends and, when needed, our backup. The town's two biggest employers were pearling and the Demco meat works, and in consequence, two factions laid claim to the Roey as their turf. Our faction was known as the lugger buggers, and the other mob, the meaties, worked the kill floor of the abattoir near Town Beach.

There soon developed a simmering rivalry between the two groups, especially between returning lugger crew and the many meaties who were local boys. We were always cashed up when we arrived, and in the mood to party. They resented our ostentatious displays of wealth and our bizarre drinking rituals, conduct which had a mesmerising effect on the local beauties (or so we liked to think).

Race played a role in fomenting this social discord. Broome had a long history of mixed race relations, including a sorry apartheid phase when harshly enforced legal restrictions controlled imported Asian labour and the movement of indigenous people. Not surprisingly, there were still underlying tensions in the local community whenever it was perceived that uppity whites were attempting to assert superiority. This apprehension was not helped by the fact that it was still quite common in some establishments for locals to be given a hard time; they would be left to wait to order, and then to wait some more for their meals or drinks. (I experienced this directly during the research for this book, when I gathered together a group of Broome women, some of them prominent citizens, and took them out to lunch at a hotel – not the Roey.)

Five luggers and Paspaley's Gumboot spelt fifty thirsty crewmen, and apart from the two Japanese boats and the *Paspaley I*, the luggers were almost entirely 'all white' crew. The Japanese would sometimes join us, particularly on the first night in port, but overall they tended to drink in the privacy of their quarters. In disagreements with the locals, we had the unwavering support of the two Papuan divers off the *Paspaley I*, Akiri and Cheb, who acted as community mediators. Cheb had fearsome facial tattoos and a build which would have made him a worthy rival to Mike Tyson. His entry into any dispute was almost guaranteed to end in the aggressor's total submission. The Thursday Islanders based at Kuri Bay and on the PPL mother ships also tended to side with lugger crew in any confrontation, and handy allies they were too.

There was seldom a dull moment at the Roey. One weekend, several elderly gentlemen residents of Kennedy Hill, the Aboriginal community located on the real estate behind the hotel, decided to give a spear throwing demonstration. They were somewhat fortified when they began their exhibition, a competition for distance using Dampier Terrace as a firing range.

The first warning to drinkers in the front bar was the clattering on the iron roof of a volley of wayward spears. There was no malice intended. I was watching from the Sandfly apartments, as we called Steve Arrow's place across the road from the pub; the whole episode was hilarious. Such was not the view of the police who arrived, sirens wailing, to put an immediate stop to this spontaneous outbreak of indigenous athletics.

On other occasions things were a little more serious. When several truckloads of people from the desert community of Balgo arrived in town in 1980, fights erupted between them and the local Bardi and other coastal language groups. The desert visitors quickly got the upper hand, and about fifty Balgo men and supporters then turned their attention to the Roebuck, from which several of their clan had been evicted.

This happened on a Sunday, traditionally one of the best lubricated days of the week at the Roey. Tensions had been brewing for most of the afternoon. By the time they cooked off in earnest, many police were off duty, and those working quickly found themselves outnumbered and forced to take cover inside the front bar of the Alamo. What followed turned into a celebrated siege as a riot raged outside the pub and a police van was overturned. Carl Sputore recalled: 'By then the mob were milling around outside gathering whatever they could find to use as weapons. The situation was definitely getting ugly. I was given guard duty for both the pub's side and back entrances but they did not try a flanking attack, possibly because I had Terry Cullen's German shepherd, Rommel, on a close leash. The crowd concentrated a full assault on the front verandah.'

Although it was after closing time, those inside found themselves trapped. Carl again: 'I have an image of Knoxy (the barman) and others jabbing beer keg spears and pool cues through the wire grill to fend off the invaders while we were being pelted with rocks and bottles.' Norm House corroborates this version: 'Shameless Shane and Bazza Thorpe were inside the pub, fending off the Balgo boys with pool cues through the window bars. The cops had barricaded themselves inside, and would not open the door, much to the disgust of the locals.'

But Broome was not always like a bad day in Watts, Los Angeles, and if the Roey riot was race relations at its worst then there was a flip side. The aforementioned Bazza, a Tasmanian, was one of a handful of footy-mad pearling crew who played for local Aussie Rules teams, club participation that helped soothe occasional ethnic tensions and provide some indigenous role models. Brian Sahana, a burly former indigenous footy star whose Afghan forebears had driven camel teams in the Kimberley, enjoyed far-reaching influence among younger hotheads. He reminded me of Bob Hite, lead singer of the band Canned Heat, the one they nicknamed The Bear. Sahana loved a beer and tended to a comfortable posture at the bar, reposing with his T-shirt rolled up above a massive bare gut upon which was perched an ice-cold middy.

Then there were those of us who chose to do our part for interracial harmony by making love, not war. To me, Broome had some of the most attractive women I had ever set eyes on, a view shared by many of my former diving colleagues. The multicultural gene pool – a genetic lottery of Aboriginal, Thursday Islander, Chinese, Malay, Japanese, European, Timorese, Filipino, and Afghan – had evolved an exotic local beauty. Friendships leading to romance blossomed quickly between many of the local indigenous women and lugger crew, a tradition spanning generations in which I and most of my diving mates were shameless and enthusiastic participants.

In 1979 there was no dispute that local women ruled the dance floor at the Roebuck Bay Hotel, both in number and style. Timing was critical to guarantee a fun night at the Roey. Lugger crew preferred to arrive back in port on Fridays or Saturdays when the pub was at its rocking best, packed with a crowd of noisy revellers including an abundance of unattached young women. Terry Cullen would order extra bar staff whenever we were back from a neap, partly because the lugger crew tended to draw a lot of friends and followers to the hotel.

A typical night might start with a crew dinner at any of a handful of Broome's Chinese restaurants, Wings, Fongs, Tongs or – if you were in a hurry – a legendary long soup at Tang Wei's café. Then it was down to serious business. A good session often lasted two days or more. 'Jacko', Mick Bray and Selby Isles off Allan Badger's lugger B-3 liked to take the edge off with several jugs of 'martini'. This was my first encounter with a high-octane cocktail and its cumulative effect on the human condition over the course of an evening was impressive.

Coming in from one neap in a generous mood, I asked a bemused barmaid at the Roey to make seventy-six Harvey Wall Bangers, a shout which I am assured has never been repeated. That lunatic gesture cost me more than $200, and a massive hangover to add to the pain of an empty wallet the next morning.

Then there was the time that visiting adman John Singleton decided to film one of our wild evenings in the pub for a documentary he was making. At the end, he put an open tab on the bar. No one went home thirsty.

In the pursuit of an alcoholic equivalent of avgas nothing came close to a concoction we dubbed a 'Communist Plot', a double shot of every white spirit available from the bar, plus a hint of red grenadine, mixed in a jug and topped with either a splash of tonic or soda. The resulting hangover defied description. It was after a night on the 'plots' that I found myself at McDaniel's, the former grand residence of a once mighty Broome pearler whose name was carried by our lugger, the *DMcD* (or *Dan McDaniel*). The place, which had been much better looked after than the Palace, was now rented out to long-term residents of the responsible variety.

Only fragments of memory survive the night. I was with Steve Zimmerle and Kevin Piper, in attendance at a party which was held in the room of someone who was absent from Broome. Another acquaintance called Mossie, a self-styled jack of all trades who had worked as a deckhand for one neap on our boat, insisted that he demonstrate his fire breathing prowess. We readily agreed. Taking a huge draft from a bottle of methylated spirits he attempted to atomise the volatile fuel mix by blowing the spray through pursed lips while holding a cigarette lighter under the volatile spray.

Unfortunately his lung power ran out before the contents had been expelled, and what had started as a spectacular rendition of a fire-breathing dragon was in seconds transformed into a human torch as Mossie coughed and spluttered the residual fuel over his chest.

There was a moment of stunned silence as we attempted to comprehend the flaming apparition in front of us, then Zimmo tore down a nearby curtain to extinguish him. We dropped Mossie off at Broome Hospital where he was treated for shock and minor burns. I say 'dropped off' because he was deposited in a semi-catatonic state on the roadside outside the hospital, none of us being too keen on having to explain to the matron the circumstances leading to his injuries.

When our absent friend returned to Broome, he was furious that we had inadvertently started a blaze in his room. In retrospect, we could have accidentally burnt down the place. Fortunately, given my history as a Broome heritage activist, it still stands today there in Weld Street, now more than 110 years old, a fine example of tropical bungalow style as its heritage assessment says, with lattice, louvres, and shutters, surrounded by a tropical garden.

THE LAST PEARLING LUGGER

Once our two-day holiday was over and we began preparing to go to sea again, we still managed to spend a fair bit of time in the Roey. Whenever I was on the *DMcD*, at least once a season we would careen her in the narrow creek channel for anti-fouling, a smelly, filthy chore in the foetid, sandfly-infested mangrove swamp. The job involved lying the boat on her side, then scrubbing the hull clean and applying a coat of highly toxic paint to protect against algae and marine growth. With one side of the hull done we would adjourn to the Roey to enjoy several hours of cold drinks before the tide turned.

Sandflies, difficult to see with the naked eye, inevitably hunted in swarms. They left a rash of red, stinging lesions across the belly, the elbows, forearms and ankles – anywhere that had been exposed during the work of painting. If scratched, the bites tended to become infected, and took weeks to heal. Having done our best in the Roey's front bar to inoculate ourselves against the swarming infestations down in the swamp, we would stagger back down Dampier Terrace to the jetty, lay the lugger on her opposite side and repeat the process. At the end of the day we emerged covered head to toe in paint, mangrove slime and painful bites.

Most of our evenings at the pub ended in a 'shout for Groper Gill'. This was a huge stuffed groper which hung on the bar wall. Caught by TC in the Roebuck Deeps, the beast had been stuffed as a trophy and mounted. We called it Groper Gill after the tax commissioner of the day, and threw all our small change at its mouth when closing time was sounded.

CHAPTER 10

At sea on the B-3

Leg and lung power are the main physical requirements for pearl diving. The other prerequisites are quick reflexes and a practised eye to spot pearl shell lying on the bottom, camouflaged in marine growth with barely a hint of exposed mantle.

Before the boats set sail each season, the pearl divers are required to submit to the annual ritual of the medical exam. If a diver fails to obtain a clean bill of health from the Broome Hospital, the fisheries department may withhold his pearl diving licence under the 1922 Pearling Act.

In 1980, the medical exam was a fairly cursory affair: X-rays of joints and long bones, eye and ear tests, weight and respiratory checks, plus a couple of minutes hopping up and down off a stool. I cannot remember anyone failing, though some divers were cautioned about their weight. Asthma sufferers were routinely passed as fit to dive by the Broome medicos. As long as you hadn't collapsed in a wheezing heap, you got your licence. I understand that these days the scrutiny is more thorough.

The precise wording of the antiquated Pearling Act left it unclear whether we were still entitled to the ration of opium which in the old days used to be dispensed to pearl divers to ease the pain of a case of the bends. One of my diving mates, Salty Dog, reckoned we were being dudded by the Fisheries on this point, and I tended to agree.

Nonetheless, the exam meant curtailing our licentious lifestyle at least temporarily, in order to ensure a relative level of basic fitness. A week before I was due for my medical I joined a group of dune runners. We did alternate running in soft sand, switching between jogging and sprints, before undertaking a ten-kilometre jog along Cable Beach from the caravan park to Gantheaume Point and back. Perhaps this made us fitter. It certainly made us feel unusually virtuous. When I undertook the exam, the X-rays of the lungs of a heavy smoking colleague highlighted to me the effects of long-term smoking, sufficient inducement for me to give up the gaspers, save for the odd surreptitious puff.

With my licence in hand, and diving experience at Port Smith behind me, I was finally offered work with the PPL fleet when a vacancy came up on Allan Badger's lugger, *John Louis*, more commonly known as the B-3, her fleet registration. My little green diving log book records that I signed on 'July 30, 1980 – Deck Hand/Diver', so the season was well advanced by the time I stepped aboard.

THE LAST PEARLING LUGGER

The head diver was Mick Bray, a veteran of the neaps. A forty-a-day smoker who loved his beer topped with a diet of steak sandwiches, Mick usually needed to shed a few kilos of lay-up season blubber before the fleet went back to sea. Every year, about two weeks before he presented at Broome Hospital, he would start his self-designed training program. It involved wearing two black plastic garbage bags over his footy shorts while he went for endurance runs through the sandhills along Cable Beach, hard going anywhere on the coast but in Broome's tropical mid-summer near insanity, at least to my thinking. Day after day, there he was, pounding through the dunes.

Mick, a former spear fisherman, had first signed on to the B-3 crew in 1972, along with Badger, Les Seimeyck, Phil Wayne and Jimmy Everett. In those days, the white divers were just beginning to challenge the dominance of the Japanese, and there were still a few Japanese divers using the hard-hat. Mick remembered the basic conditions on board the B-3: 'We cooked on a small gas camping stove. That was it! We used to keep the fresh meat in an esky – it would last four or five days, then it was canned tucker, and then we'd spear a fish and it'd be rice and fish. There were no fresh veggies just canned.

'I would cook cottage pie out of tinned dog (corned beef) and Deb mashed potato. Back then I slept in the engine room. There were two small berths either side of the motor. It was fucking hot and noisy, and I was always having to clear spanners and shit off my bed before I could crawl in.'

Those were the days before the decks on the luggers were raised to increase the headroom. It was not a comfortable boat on which to find yourself trying to skirt the edge of a cyclone. On one neap back in the early seventies, bad weather forced the B-3 to return to port after only a few days fishing off the Eighty Mile. 'We ran huge swells coming back, and she nearly did a 360. One wave buried us. We're all standing down the back drenched in our wetsuits,' Mick recalled. 'The masts were at about 45 degrees and the wheelhouse and deck were under. Don't ask me how we came back up – we couldn't believe we had managed it. The wind and tide had gone crazy.'

By the time I signed on, I already knew the B-3 crew well: Mick, my friend Wayne House, and a former Newcastle journalist, Dave Appleby, were all good friends, and numbered among the heroic drinkers club at the Roebuck. Just as on the *DMcD*, every crew member had a nickname. Mick was and still is known as Super Fart, Wayne was Wonder Dog, Wowser or Wandoo, Dave was Applejack, and I was Doddy. Dave and Wayne were the two gun divers, ferocious rivals for the 'King of the Neap' title, the diver with the biggest shell tally. The skipper was Badger. He was a former world champion spear fisherman with two obsessions, ice-cream and margarine, which he slathered in liberal dollops on all his food.

Work on the PPL fleet luggers was easier than the *DMcD*, but the ship had a strict routine. I began as a spare diver, cook/deckhand and tender – the latter duties shared with the seemingly mild mannered Badger, Norm the engineer, and Spud, a young deckhand and spare diver.

At this time, the fleet did not fish deep water. We mostly worked at a depth of 15 to 22 metres and our main job was to gather wild shell for cultured pearl cultivation.

Historic Streeters Jetty, Chinatown in Broome, 1979. This shot was taken from atop the main mast of the *DMcD* and shows three other Pearls Pty Ltd luggers.

The *DMcD*, easing her way up the narrow channel towards Streeters Jetty. We would come in on the high tide and, unless we were planning to berth alongside, we got our work done quickly to allow a timely exit.

Historic Bishop's Palace was demolished in 1979 and replaced by a block of brick units, despite local protests. My room was on the left by the open shutter.

It looks like a ghost town but it was siesta time or 'high noon' in Chinatown, 1979. The only institution open during the siesta was the famous Roebuck Bay Hotel.

Off Town Beach in 1979, the *DMcD* B-5 (Broome 5) after the massive twelve-tonne trip. Note the scarring on the side of the boat under the diving ladder caused by heaving up work bags full of pearl shell.

In comes the new. The *Paspaley I* – a modified tuna boat built of fibreglass in Japan. Compared with the luggers it could stay out longer, carry more crew, hold more live shell and had toilets and hot showers.

LEFT: Still in their wetsuits, B-6 divers Steve Oats and Larry House are hard at work shelling and cleaning, helped by Gordo the cook just out of shot.

RIGHT: Pearl shell muscle drying in the sun. They were sold to markets in Hong Kong, attracting premium prices as an aphrodisiac.

RIGHT: A storm front approaches. The *DMcD* had an open stern console that offered little protection from the elements during a typical two- to three-hour watch.

LEFT: *DMcD* head diver, John 'The Colonel' Stewart, checking bags of mother-of-pearl. On this trip we fished eight tonnes of mother-of-pearl and several thousand live shell, which were kept for pearl cultivation.

Assorted pearling crew at the Roey. *Left to right*: Steve Arrow (*DMcD*), Dave Jackson (*Paspaley I*), Wayne House (*John Louis*, B-3), Geoff Ward (cook/deckhand on the *Roebuck Pearl*), the author (B-3), Russell Hanigan (*Paspaley I* skipper), Bruce Barker, Judy Arrow, Mick Bray (head diver B-3), his girlfriend Pauline, Liz, and Richard Baillieu (*Roebuck Pearl* diver).

Off-duty pearl divers at the Roey. *Left to right*: Norm House (seated with head turned away), the author (with cigarette), Paspaley diver, the late Chebastio and the late Barry Thorpe, then diving for Broome Pearls.

RIGHT: *DMcD* head deckhand, Mark Feeney in 1979. Tough as nails Feeney would work the pearling season then head south to Geraldton and work a second season on the crayfishing boats.

LEFT: *DMcD* head diver John Stewart; affable and friendly, pictured here with a highly venomous sea snake.

LEFT: One of the denizens of the deep retrieved while drifting the Eighty Mile; commonly known as a 'monkey fish'.

LEFT: *DMcD* crewmates in 1983, Shane Ford and Cossack use a block and tackle to manually heave up dump bags of shell on a prolific patch off the Eighty Mile.

RIGHT: The bush camp on Suburban Road was home for Ramah and me for several months before we found rented accommodation back in town. It was an enchanting interval far from the madding crowd.

LEFT: One birthday I bought an eighteen-gallon keg and installed it on the back of my Land Cruiser. After a day of mayhem we ended up bogged in sand hills on Cable Beach, so we slept in the sand. We felt no pain.

LEFT: On a trip up to One Arm Point, I helped Ramah's indigenous relatives butcher a leatherback turtle. These days all marine turtles are experiencing serious threats to their survival, but this one was legally fished by locals and the meat distributed.

RIGHT: B-6 diver Steve Oats, seen here preparing to dive.

RIGHT: The late Barry 'Bazza' Thorpe (centre), diver and Tasmanian wildman, whose idea of fun during the spring tide interval ashore was a bout of bare knuckle boxing with Maori Nick.

LEFT: Chopping 'commies' or commercial pearl shell while working as deckie/spare diver on the PPL lugger *John Louis* B-3. *Left to right*: the author, Norm the engineer and Spud, another deckie.

RIGHT: The resident king of mayhem, Shameless Shane Ford in 1983. A talented diver, mechanic and engineer, he once famously cut the top off his girlfriend's Toyota Corolla sedan.

LEFT: My old art school mate Gary Proctor in acute pain after being pierced by the spike of a 'dream fish' on board Broome Pearls' *Pacific Lady*.

Happier days onboard the PPL lugger *Buccleuch* (B-6). *Left to right*: Steve Oats, the author, Dave Jackson, Larry House, skipper Alan Nunn, Mark Walsh and Gordon Byers.

Good times were always had at a Shinju Matsuri (Festival of the Pearl) Ball, held at the Broome Civic Centre. The author, in a very mellow mood, with girlfriend Ramah.

The late Akari Wosomo from Daru in PNG, one of Paspaley's top divers at a legendary Shinju Ball.

LEFT: The author with a handsome painted crayfish caught while diving off the *Pacific Lady*.

RIGHT: Wayne 'Wonder Dog' standing on the lugger diving ladder. Wonder worked occasionally on the *DMcD* after completing a season for PPL on board the fleet lugger B-3 *John Louis*. Along with his younger brother Larry ('Wonder Pup'), Wayne had a reputation as one of the strongest pearl divers in Broome. Like many pearling crew members, he cut his teeth in the crayfishing industry.

A Thursday Island worker tends to cultured shell attached to baskets hanging from a raft moored off Beagle Bay, part of a Barrow Pearls lease north of Broome. The *DMcD* is anchored just offshore.

LEFT: Steve Arrow in 1983 practicing the technique of round pearl cultivation at the pearl farm at Beagle Bay. The technique was eventually perfected, breaking a critical dependence on Japanese technicians.

A rare natural pearl; an almost flawless gem found on the *DMcD* in 1979.

THE LAST PEARLING LUGGER

The *Kuri Pearl* and *Merinda Pearl* would arrive in shifts. Their Torres Strait crews would run a dinghy shuttle to the luggers, to collect the shell which the mother ships would then transfer to the farm at Kuri Bay, 420 kilometres north of Broome.

Commercial shell too large or old for cultured pearls was also collected to be harvested for its mother-of-pearl, but we fished it in nothing like the quantities we had when I was working on the *DMcD*. At the end of a neap we would berth alongside Streeters Jetty and the sacks of mother-of-pearl would be unloaded and taken to the sorting shed to be graded and consigned to Gerdau in New York.

For the divers, life onboard involved constant attempts to finesse our equipment. Wetsuits were a particular source of grievance. The choice of suits was limited, so we all welcomed an offer to try a new type of made-to-measure number known as the Star Diver or Star suit, which was constructed of soft rubber rather than the traditional foam neoprene material which resulted in painful welts. The new suit was promoted by one of the Japanese lugger crew, Hiro, one of the last of the Japanese hard-hat divers who had set himself up as import agent for a wetsuit company specialising in tailor-made rubber. Unlike the 'blue heeler', the Star suit was smooth with welded seams, but because it was thin rubber required great care when fitting.

Any suit copped a hammering during the season and most divers ended up looking like rag dolls by the time that the quota was fished, their suits patchworks of rubber. More than one diver was forced to glue his suit back together after dressing too hastily in the dawn light on a rocking lugger deck. It was important to first lubricate the suit with water. The most convenient method was jamming a deck hose into the sleeve and suffering a momentary blast of icy sea water while you wriggled into the suit. In choppy seas with a sou'easter blowing this was easier said than done. Another method involved pouring a solution of shampoo and warm water into the suit to minimise friction and tearing. It was initially more comfortable than the deck hose, but caused lousy skin rashes that took days to clear.

The Star suits had a tighter fit than the neoprene 'blue heelers'. They were more comfortable and certainly kept the wearer warmer for longer. But as they were manufactured in Japan, it was vital when ordering to ensure that your measurements were listed correctly. One season Wonder got his measurements mixed up and in trying to force his not inconsiderable bulk into the tight garment only managed to tear the rubber to shreds. At first we commiserated. The Star suits were expensive, and it looked like a terrible waste of money. With several tubes of Tarzan's Grip the problem was fixed, though when Wonder finally got his suit on, it looked as though he had just caught a full frontal mortar blast.

The fleet master was an old hard-hat diver called Takada, and the two Australian skippered luggers tended to follow him and fish wherever his flagship, the lugger B-1, went. At the start of the year we would usually dive in shallow water in close off False Cape Bossut or 'potato' country near Mangrove Point, before moving steadily south with each consecutive neap.

Inshore around seven fathoms meant the visibility was usually poor. The first dives in the early morning were best, after which visibility deteriorated. The positive side to diving in shallow water was that it allowed long drifts without having to worry too much about decompression.

While the pace of work was easier than on the *DMcD*, the B-3's skipper was a stickler for rules and routine. He was also the most safety conscious and the most authoritative when it came to diving medicine. His lugger was the first to carry pethidine and Phenergan, which were used in case of stings from the dreaded irukandji, a tiny jellyfish whose tentacles become extremely toxic during the warm months, though they are less so when the water is colder.

The irukandji was our main danger during diving operations but it was not the only marine nasty to confront. As we drifted along the bottom sea snakes would follow us for hours. It was an unnerving experience to look behind and sight a two-metre sea snake meandering hypnotically in your wake, propelled by its distinctive flat paddle tail.

Hanging onto your work line, you would float like an astronaut over a large coral cup and watch a hibernating snake wrapped up like coiled rope suddenly unwind and start falling in behind you, its tiny beady black eyes fixed on your flippers. The Papuan Akiri Wosomo, a top diver, once got out of the water and refused to enter it again for the rest of the neap when a snake started following him. He believed it was a reincarnation of a grandfather with whom he had never got along: there was no way he was going back in the water to fish pearl shell.

The sea snake's venom is more toxic than the worst land snake, and contrary to a popular misconception, they are not hindered by their small mouths, because they can dislocate their jaw in order to swallow prey, mostly fish, three or four times the diameter of their neck. Sometimes sea snakes attracted by the sediment stirred up by our flippers would get inside divers' work bags or wrap themselves along the work lines for a ride, but they were seldom aggressive. Though I noticed they became far more active during their mating season, I have never heard of one fatally biting a pearl diver.

Outcrops of reef tended to attract shoals of fish which in turn attracted bigger fish all the way up the food chain past pearl divers until you got to the ultimate evolutionary munching machine, sharks. We saw sand sharks, carpet sharks, docile wobbegongs, reef sharks, black-tip whalers, bronze whalers, makos, tigers and hammerheads but, thankfully, in our part of the world, no great whites, the shark most likely to kill humans.

There were always big sharks around when we were diving, attracted by our activity in the water. You might never see them but you sure felt the proximity vibe. They were never far away, lurking in the gloom where the zone of visibility faded into light dappled murk. Your dive buddy would let you know all about it back on deck at the end of a drift.

'Hey Doddy, you had a 12-foot bronze whaler check you out ten minutes into that last dive,' Wonder Dog nonchalantly told me on one occasion.

His sanguine cheeriness made me think that if a big one had your name you would know nothing until the moment it clamped its dental formula around your torso: just a few microseconds of pure terror before all consciousness was extinguished in the process of transformation into human berley.

Estimating size underwater can be tricky due to the magnification effect of the diving mask – about twenty-five per cent – and that includes everything from pearl shell to predators. Nevertheless, we would occasionally catch a glimpse of something bigger than other sharks, a flash of light off the pectoral fin of a tiger shark. That was all you would see – just a glance of something enormous. Tigers grow up to five metres, and are the second most likely shark species to attack, after the great white. A tiger sighting was enough to put the frighteners on you for the rest of the day.

Sharks seldom stuck around for long, just enough time to scope you out as a potential meal; with a couple of pumps of their tails they were gone at warp speed. But it was especially spooky at night, when tigers like to feed. I used to get the shits 'hanging off'. This was our preventive against the bends, decompressing the nitrogen build-up in our bodies by staying submerged at the end of a long day's diving. It was freezing cold in the water as I watched jellyfish drift overhead in the fading light, and tried not to think of what was swimming underneath. Any unthinking crewman who tossed offal or dinner scraps over during a hang-off would almost certainly risk getting their lights punched out.

It was off the Monte Bellos in 1980 that Big Bag had an encounter with a giant hammerhead and had to fend it off with the iron hoop of his shell bag as the monster circled him inquisitively. Bruce took up smoking after that. Squire joked that he saw Big Bag on deck with three fags jammed between his fingers after his run-in with old hammerhead. 'Mate, it was like something out of *Star Wars* – two fucking eyes each end of this great set of choppers,' Big Bag told me in his own defence.

There were other nasties, tiny toxic critters like the dream fish which could inject a lethal sting through your diving glove as you struggled to tear an old clunker off the bottom. The aptly named bearded ghoul, or Devil Fish, would leave exposed skin looking like it had just been flailed with a cat-o'-nine-tails. Then there was the bandy-bandy, an aggro little sea snake less than a foot long, with a penchant for launching suicidal attacks on your face mask.

Our good mate Salty Dog started collecting nasty marine critters for his aquarium of aquatic horror. Divers competed to find the most poisonous and deadliest denizens of the deep for this collection. Before too long Salty had small sharks, sea snakes, dream fish, cone shells, blue-ringed octopus, box jellyfish, irukandji stingers and stonefish.

It was a noxious puddle of poison that held pride of place at The Kennels, a legendary crash pad for a group of hard-core divers, including Salty Dog, Wayne's younger brother Wonder Pup, and Steve Oats from Paspaley. Back in port for a spring, over the course of an evening and several bottles of Jack Daniels, innumerable beers and enough green flake aromatic to sedate an elephant, we would observe the interaction of these little beasties, a delectable revenge on our tormenters in the big aquarium off the Eighty Mile. To us at least, it was a highly amusing spectacle as these toxic avengers slugged it out in a gladiatorial fight to the death which eventually wiped out all contestants.

✢ ✢ ✢

THE LAST PEARLING LUGGER

As the season progressed, the fleet drifted steadily south from the potato country, working traditional grounds in close to the shore, pearl shell patches with names like the 'Land of the Yellow Weed' or the 'Lost World of Wallal'. At 10 fathoms (20 metres), the water became noticeably clearer for longer, which was a godsend for me because, compared with many other divers, I was hopeless at spotting pearl shell in the murky shallows of potato country. Nevertheless, my confidence as a diver was building, and by now I felt totally comfortable in the water despite all the paraphernalia we had to wear. I learnt to clean my mask under water using a sea sponge torn off the bottom.

When I wasn't diving I worked on deck or in the galley. By now I had learnt to cook a reasonable roast chicken, beef curry and shepherd's pie. Bray's speciality was sweet and sour fish.

I was thankful that at least Badger had figured out that a working freezer was a necessity on a lugger. In contrast to the ice box on the *DMcD*, the deep freeze on the B-3 actually worked. It made me wonder if Farley was so old school that he thought refrigeration was a luxury. I reckon the only difference between the tucker on the *DMcD* and the First Fleet was (a) the invention of Vitamin C tablets to ward off scurvy and (b) Farley's mackerel mornay. One thing never changed whether you were aboard the B-3 or the *DMcD*: bread could only be stored for three or four days before it went mouldy.

We lived for food. Swimming burnt off loads of calories and required three square meals a day, usually with second and third helpings washed down with a hot brew and a beer night cap. By the time all the shell bags were packed, deck cleaned, hoses coiled up and dinner plates washed we were just about ready for the snore box. Sometimes Badger would get his banjo out and strum a few tunes. Unlike Squire, whose plucking had driven us all to the point of insanity on the *DMcD*, Badger was relatively accomplished on the instrument.

I enjoyed that season on a PPL lugger, not to mention the extra dollars it brought in. Because the PPL skippers were all too aware that their boats paid the best wages, they could afford to be selective in hiring crew, which ensured most divers and crew would put up with personality quirks of the skipper that might otherwise have resulted in a bit of lip. Badger was generally a good boss, but he could have his moments, and one came at the end of a humid windless afternoon. I was alternating as diver deckhand and had just finished chopping shell and packing. Feeling very thirsty, I headed off for a foam water container which I knew was down the stern.

The divers were just coming up and Badger spotted me. He yelled out at me thinking I was drinking directly from the container. In fact I was pouring the water into my parched gullet. Irritated by this injustice, I fired back: 'What do you think I've got? Foot and mouth disease?' Gobbing off at the skipper did not go down well and I was quietly informed later by some of the other divers that my remarks had rankled and Badger was unimpressed.

He said nothing to me after that and by the next neap I thought the whole thing had been forgotten. Then one morning as we prepared to set the drogue for a drift for the first dive of the day, someone called out that a rope had tangled around the propeller. I was preparing to dive,

THE LAST PEARLING LUGGER

and was already dressed in my long johns, though I hadn't yet pulled on my wetsuit top. Instinctively, I checked to ensure the gear box was not engaged, before grabbing a deck knife and goggles and diving overboard to cut the tangle of rope off the prop.

It only took a minute. Job done, I resurfaced and clambered back on board, thinking that Badger would thank me and then we would get started diving. How wrong I was. The skipper remained ominously quiet, but Super Fart later warned me to 'prepare for the worst', because I had broken one of Badger's golden rules. He was referring to the skipper's policy that nobody was allowed to dive without being completely covered up because of the danger posed by the irukandji stingers that were prevalent in the water at that time of the year. I was outraged. To my mind, I was innocent of anything except trying to help out, and, though I had acted on impulse, no harm had come from it.

With our quota fished, the fleet was ready for the lay-up. As we turned for home at the end of the neap, Super Fart told me he had tried to convince Badger of the mitigating circumstances. This didn't sound promising. Motoring back into port, I suddenly felt distinctly gloomy.

Back in Broome, I was asked to collect my pay. I drove around to Badger's house with my girlfriend, Ramah. There was no way I would be begging to keep the job, I told her.

CHAPTER 11

Ramah and friends

Ramah was a Broome girl through and through, the daughter of a Malay former pearling worker and a local Bardi woman.

When we first met, she was going out with a deckie I knew. Though that relationship met a natural end, she and her friends continued to be part of our group. Eventually Ramah and I connected at an impromptu party behind Cable Beach, convened around my Land Cruiser which had become hopelessly bogged in the sand dunes with a keg of beer conveniently parked on the back.

We moved in together a month or so later, and stayed together for almost three years. Who knows how long we might have lasted had I not eventually wanted to leave

Broome, while she inevitably wanted to stay. I found that people who were born in Broome usually had no desire to leave the town permanently.

Ramah was a few years younger than me, not tall, but sexy and full of life. Her eyes were brown, her features recognisably Malay, with prominent cheekbones and a wide smile. She was hard working and resilient, with a cheeky sense of humour. When we first got together she was staffing the Avis office in Derby. It was a very busy depot, with tourists and miners and other visiting businessmen constantly needing cars and four-wheel drives. She was on call, and spent a lot of her time delivering vehicles from Broome to Derby and vice versa.

Later, when I returned to the *DMcD*, Ramah came along too, as cook and deckie. At the time, she was the only woman on the lugger. There were no shower facilities and no toilets on the boat. You relieved yourself by hanging your arse over the stern during a quiet moment, and bathed by tossing a bucket of water over yourself on deck. I wondered how she would cope first time out, but Ramah never grumbled about the primitive living conditions and her personality was robust enough to stand the salty exchanges that passed for conversation among a crew that included the likes of Shameless. She could also handle the occasional brusque command from the skipper, Big Bag, or the time he questioned her judgement when she purchased a two-litre jar of vegemite for the boat.

One day Ramah stubbed her big toe on the shell-strewn deck, and soon it was badly swollen. In great pain, she hobbled around on deck continuing to work until she could no longer walk. The neap was far from over, and there was no question of returning to port for an infected toe, so Big Bag took the matter in hand with his usual resourcefulness. As delicately as he could, he drilled through her black, rotting nail with a power tool to relieve the pressure and allow the wound to drain. Radical but practical!

Afterwards, whenever new crew began whingeing about work conditions Barker used to shame them with the example of her stoicism, laying it on with a trowel. 'Ramah was in pain – but *she* never cried,' he told them.

We did manage nights together on the lugger when I was on watch duty and I always got a laugh watching dinghies from the other luggers ferry overnight companions ashore at first light.

Ashore, she always seemed to be surrounded by people. Besides her mum and dad and siblings, there were her mother's people up at Cape Leveque, the northernmost point of the Dampier Peninsula, 220 kilometres north of Broome up a dusty, corrugated track. Then there were her many indigenous friends in town. We all enjoyed fishing, camping and partying. Through Ramah I gained an entrée into the indigenous world of Broome, an aspect of the town's life that I would have otherwise only glimpsed from the sidelines. Her circle opened up insights into Aboriginal experience and culture that I would otherwise never have had. Years before I ever heard the term 'stolen children', these people told me stories of indigenous children being taken away from their parents. It was hard to believe when I first heard it, but similar stories would come up over and over.

On a beautiful coastline, Cape Leveque is a particularly beautiful spot, its white sand beaches studded by red sand buttes blown into weird shapes by the wind. Its blue-green seas at the sometimes wild entrance to King Sound are matched by peaceful coves perfect for fishing, swimming and snorkelling. Whenever we used to head up there, I was amazed at the difference between Ramah the town girl – quick, efficient and full of plans – and Ramah at Cape Leveque, a girl utterly at ease with her surroundings, relaxed so completely that she would fish all day without running out of patience. She loved to throw out a line, and once I taught her a better technique she and her girlfriends were probably more successful at it than me and my mates. Friends and family showed us their fishing spots, and we repaid them with some of the catch. Mackerel and sailfish were prolific, and easy to catch from a dinghy at sea, trevally and bream were more likely off the beach and along Hunters Creek.

One day in Broome, just returned from sea, I opened the fridge door at home to discover, coiled up on a dinner plate, a freshly gutted lizard, a present from Auntie 'One Eye' from Cape Leveque. She had been visiting town and wanted to leave a token of appreciation for a parcel of fresh fish we had left with her family during a spear fishing and camping trip with Walshy and his girlfriend, Amy, and Norm and Karen.

Hunters Creek, on the northeast side of the cape, had a dark history involving two white men named 'Frenchy' D'Antoine and Harry Hunter, who in the 1880s lived rough in a bush camp on the creek. From their camp the pair earnt a reputation for blackbirding, the selling of Aborigines to master pearlers for use as indentured labourers – slavery by any other name. D'Antoine and Hunter kept numerous girlfriends and 'wives,' who over the years bore them many children.

Several of their offspring were still alive and living in Broome when I went there. I had met two of them, brothers Chris and Robin Hunter. One Sunday afternoon at the Roebuck Bay Hotel I noticed a pair of old blokes toiling up from Morgans Camp, a collection of shacks just out of the tide line behind the PPL lugger workshops. Their gait was laboured, but as I soon found out, they rarely failed to make it to the pub for their regular session. The taller of the two had pale rheumy eyes, opaque with cataracts. His companion wore a battered old black woollen skipper's cap embroidered with a faded white anchor.

They always drank in the 'other' public bar, the exclusive domain of many of Broome's indigenous drinkers. Just a few paces separated this bar from the one favoured by white divers and deckies, but stepping into the locals' bar was like stepping into a parallel universe – a hubbub of foreign tongues, rapid-fire Aboriginal dialects, Malay and Torres Strait pidgin English.

Among the company the brothers kept I could see they were treated with respect. Modest imbibers, they drank their beer from five-ounce glasses. They had been hard-hat divers and part of the industry when it was at its rollicking peak, a time when the first primitive engines were being fitted to luggers, when sail was giving way to mechanical power. Both of them had survived ferocious storms that lashed the early pearling fleets fishing the Eighty Mile and the northern Lacepedes. Chris recalled in graphic detail how he once watched a lugger shattered into matchwood during a cyclonic storm in Roebuck Bay.

They talked of what it was like to suffer the bends in the days when diving medicine was still in its infancy. They told me that the opium ration divers were entitled to was administered not just for the pain of the bends, but to stave off the urge to defecate once they were suited up. Some things about lugger life never changed. Cockroach infestations and plagues of rats were just as big a problem in my day as in theirs.

Aboriginal people's relationship with pearling and pearl shell was complex. Before the arrival of Europeans, pearl oysters were a useful food source and trading commodity among the five main Aboriginal tribes living close to The Eighty Mile, an area they called Bidyadanga. Aboriginal men used carved pearl shell as an adornment in traditional ceremonies and pearl shell proved a handy tablet for the tribe to record important events. Northwest pearl shell has been found as far as the Great Australian Bight in the south to eastern Boulia in Queensland, evidence of Aboriginal trading routes. The creation of the northwest pearling industry was spurred on when in 1861 Aboriginals near Nichol Bay traded pearl shell with members of an exploration team led by Augustus Gregory.

Yet young Aboriginal people were kidnapped and forced to work as free divers. By 1873, faced with a scandal, the colonial government legislated against the use of women and children in the industry. World War II helped change the status of Aboriginal divers, because of the government's reluctance to allow the Japanese to return to Broome. After decades of systemic abuse they suddenly found themselves being treated with new-found respect, Roy Wiggan, a Bardi man who worked as a diver from 1949 to 1966, told me: 'We were treated equally by the Japanese and Malays, but Aboriginal divers were the best. We were better than anyone else. We could read the clouds, the sky and the sea not by using a barometer. We could tell by the colour, every detail. If a cyclone was coming the water would turn green. All this knowledge is gone now.'

* * *

THE CAPE Leveque side of Ramah's family was a complete contrast to her father's background. Early in our relationship, Ramah and I travelled to Southeast Asia: to Burma, which I had wanted to see for a long time (my Orwell obsession again), but also to Malaysia and Singapore. In some ways, her Malay connection was as alien to Ramah as it was to me. In Kota Bharu, a deeply Muslim city in northeastern Malaysia, we were walking through a market, when a woman ran toward us screaming at Ramah, rebuking her for the way she was dressed (which was not especially revealing – just the usual light clothing tourists favour). In Singapore, we stayed with Ramah's cousin in the old quarter of Geylang. He was an Islamic teacher, raising his children as devout Muslims. Every morning we would wake up to the sound of singing: Ramah's cousin was teaching his little daughters the holy songs of their faith. He joked with me about why my name was not Muhammad. No doubt he would have strongly disapproved had he realised that we were not married.

In Broome itself, 'mixed' marriages were still frowned on by 'polite' society. For a century the pearling masters had kept the coloured workforce (which far outnumbered the bosses) in its place by a combination of legal and social restrictions. State and Church frowned upon Asian workers cohabiting with Aboriginal women, even though it was a social reality. Pearl Hamaguchi, daughter of a Yawuru woman and an Asian father, was the child of one of these relationships, just as Ramah was a few decades later. Born in 1940 in Chinatown, Pearl was educated at St Mary's convent. As a young woman, she worked as a shop assistant at Streeter and Male's general store, and ended up marrying one of the Japanese who came to Broome in the late fifties for the cultured pearl industry. The couple eventually established a successful pearl farm, which they sold to the Paspaley family.

Mrs Hamaguchi vividly remembered the complexities of racial status in Broome in the fifties and sixties. It was not just the whites and the rest. Non-white society also had its social gradations: 'The Japanese were on top and the Chinese were here and the Malays were here and the Filipinos were here, and then you had the coloureds, the mixed race, and then you had the full bloods.' The young police constables who came into Streeter and Male's might give Pearl and her friends admiring gazes, but they would always be warned off if they wanted to ask her out to the Sun picture theatre on Saturday night.

Some of this feeling remained when Ramah and I were a couple. Many of the pearling fraternity regarded the mixed-race girls of Broome with fascination, but as potential sexual conquests, not friends and partners. Others

THE LAST PEARLING LUGGER

like my mate Dave Appleby and his girlfriend, Di Edgar, settled into stable long-term relationships and raised their own families. I came to know several of these women – the Tang Wei sisters, Eunice Yu and Ramah – as friends, and to admire them. They were hard working, cheeky, proud of their parents' struggle to survive and be accepted in Broome, and well aware of their own charms as well as those of their home town. Just as Ramah proved herself able to cope with the arduous macho lifestyle of the luggers, so they carved out a place for themselves in the life of Broome.

This did not mean they were kindly regarded by everyone, as I found out when I tried to rent a house. I had a double handicap. I was a pearl diver with a reputation – not entirely unjustified – for being a hellraiser, and I also had an indigenous girlfriend. This combination made finding somewhere to live difficult in the extreme. There was an old house near Town Beach which was vacant and looked perfect for us. It was owned by the shire but they declined our rental proposition. It seemed that nobody wanted to rent to us. I tried to believe that it was probably more a reflection of my tearaway reputation than some sort of judgement on our 'mixed' status. Weeks went by while we camped at Riddell Beach, waiting for a solution to appear. At one stage I even considered moving to Derby, about 200 kilometres away, and returning to Broome for the fishing neaps.

Then Dave Dureau threw us a lifeline. He owned acreage on Suburban Road and was keen to see it occupied. The block was just a sandhill away from the ocean, and had electricity and potable water on tap. Of more critical importance, the next wet season was months away so a proper campsite was a feasible option. Ramah and I gratefully accepted his offer at a peppercorn rental.

After rigging a canvas lean-to over a metal frame which we found on the block and building a rudimentary shower and a long-drop dunny, we had a home. We cooked over an open fire using a camp oven and kept our fish, meat and dairy chilled in an old car fridge. It was a simple uncomplicated lifestyle and we loved it. There was another upside as far as Ramah was concerned: the block was about 12 kilometres from town, which reduced my outings to the Roey.

The site lay close to Cable Beach, which was a real plus. By cutting a path through the scrub we would emerge over the sand dunes just north of the Naked Beach and south of Coconut Wells – our own private beach – not bad. The block was well timbered, so by day there was pleasant shade. The night skies were clear and the stars shone brightly. There was even some bush tucker, Kakadu plums, hanging from the gubinge trees on the block.

Our only real brush with discomfort came when we left our towels hooked over a low-lying tree branch while we showered. Within minutes of wiping ourselves dry we both broke out in huge, itchy red welts. It was agony. We tried hosing ourselves down but with no relief. In the end we had to rush down to Broome Hospital for injections of antihistamine.

Soon, word got out about our idyllic situation on Suburban Road and friends began to drop by. The first regular visitors to our camp were the Thursday Islanders who worked the PPL mother ships and related to our lifestyle, telling us their stories around the campfire at night over a few beers.

We lasted several months there and were the stronger as a couple for the experience. But when Norm and Karen came through with an offer to share rental digs with them, we took the chance to trade up. After all, they had managed to find a three-bedroom, furnished transportable home complete with king-size water bed. What more could a diver want?

CHAPTER 12

The season from hell

Anyway, back to my trouble with Badger. If he wanted to sack me then so be it, I told Ramah as we drove around to the skipper's. And that was exactly what happened.

'Sorry, mate, I've got to let you go,' he said, and that was the end of my career on the B-3. His wife, Delma, wrote me out a cheque.

I took the news badly, angered at what I thought was Badger's narrow-mindedness. By now I was convinced that all lugger skippers were petty tyrants and Captain Queegs. Their typical insistence that the crew follow their rules exactly seemed needlessly pedantic to a free spirit like me. The 1980 season was almost over anyway, I consoled myself, but I worried whether I would be able to find diving work the following season. Fortunately, I was offered work on Farley's *Roebuck Pearl*.

Compared with the old *DMcD* with its cramped accommodation and malfunctioning winch, the new boat was cutting edge. Based on a proven trawler design, she was about thirty metres in length, all-steel construction, with airconditioned quarters designed to accommodate more than a dozen crew members in comfort. In terms of creature comforts there were hot showers and a full-time dedicated cook, the decks were spacious, there was a hydraulic winch for the anchor, and overhead drum winches on the aft deck to assist the retrieval of heavy shell bags.

She had an experienced crew that season. I was happy to see several old faces from the *DMcD*, including Feeney. Norm had also signed up as a deckhand. The new divers included Wonder Dog's younger brother, Larry House, and Steve Oats, who had now left Paspaley. Then there was the skipper, Farley, for my money the cleverest tactician in the fleet.

We had everything going for us. Yet, in the way of these things, the early neaps of 1981 failed to deliver on the spectacular shell patches we had struck two years before. We went over old ground searching for new shell, and even made a foray north into the Lacepede Channel after scratching around off Gantheaume Point.

It was March, and because the water was still warm we tended not to wear thick heavy-duty wetsuits, preferring light surfing long johns and skivvy. Instead of my diver's hood I wore a neoprene balaclava with broad shoulder flap which had an annoying tendency to lift up in the current like a manta ray taking off.

THE LAST PEARLING LUGGER

One day, we were drifting in about twenty-four metres of water when I felt what seemed like a bee sting over my exposed jugular. The flaps on my shoulders lifted, and cool water rushed against a small exposed part of my neck as I swam toward a couple of pearl shell on the outside of my work line. Then the bee sting. I tried to convince myself it was nothing more than a piece of floating fire coral. The pain would ease in a moment, no drama, nothing to it, I told myself, just keep picking up shell.

As the minutes passed, it was clear that all was not well. I developed a worrying tingle in my lower spine, and it quickly morphed into something altogether more serious until my entire backbone felt as if it was hard-wired to a wild, surging electric current. I must have lost track of time, floating in a delusory state, for when I peered into my neck bag all I saw was clumps of seaweed that I'd been collecting instead of pearl shell.

I realised that my breathing was becoming laboured, and I was struggling for short and rapid breaths. By now, I felt as if someone was trying to saw through my spine. Then my vision began to blur.

With difficulty I reached the end of my work line, tied to the down weight which in turn was connected to another rope which travelled through a pulley tied to the outrigger. From here it should have been straight up, hand over hand, a nice and easy ascent. I wasn't lost, but my sight was shot and I was beginning to feel a stabbing pain behind my eyeballs. With my eyes closed I began a slow, methodical ascent, each hand movement progressively more difficult and uncoordinated.

I barely remember reaching the dive ladder. I think it was Larry or Norm who hauled me off the steps and by then I was fading in and out of consciousness, and vomiting uncontrollably. Just fragments of memory follow, of constant vomiting and really weird pain like nothing I had ever felt before, like hot needles being rammed into my arse, the palms of my hands, my finger tips, the back of my eyeballs. All the while, surges of 'wave' pain would sweep along my spine. I remember wondering if it was going to get any worse, because I didn't know how much more pain I could take. Not knowing was the scary part. I was worried I would die from asphyxiation because I was having so much trouble breathing. Suppressing my panic was a major challenge.

Farley came down from the wheelhouse, took one look at me, and got on the radio to my old boss Badger. If I hadn't been in so much pain, I would have appreciated the screaming irony more. The Thursday Islanders from the mother ship *Merinda Pearl* ferried me at speed back to the B-3 and Badger's tender ministrations. We crashed over the surf, the dinghy's outboard blasting at full revs. In my heightened state of sensitivity, I was overpowered by the smells of two-stroke and rotting fish filling my nostrils. At least the sea spray that blasted over the bow and drenched my face was cool and soothing. As the little runabout bumped along, hammering my agonised spine, I could hear the murmur of TI creole. None of the Islanders liked being close to someone in my crook state. It was bad juju, and they wanted me off their boat as soon as possible.

Alongside the lugger, my old crewmates Wonder, Appleby and Mick hauled me up and onto the engine hatch.

I thanked them by vomiting in their direction. By now all I could produce was foul-smelling bile. I heard Badger say: 'Doddy's got a bad one.' That really freaked me out. If Badger thought I was bad, I must be really fucked up. He shot me up with the maximum allowance of pethidine and then some, followed by a booster of antihistamine.

A few weeks before me Appleby had been stung by an irukandji, and I remembered his agony-induced bawling. I concentrated on fighting an overwhelming urge to cry: irrationally, this seemed very important. Badger and Mick asked me questions. I think they were trying to figure where I'd been stung so that they could check if there was any residual tentacle aggravating my condition. I was unable even to mouth a response. By that stage I could barely focus my eyes, let alone my brain.

Next, it was back in the dinghy and over to the *Roebuck Pearl*. Farley had turned the trawler around to ferry me back to Broome.

At last, the drugs kicked in, not killing the pain but making it more bearable. After three hours the excruciating aches and stabbing pains began to subside and my breathing became more measured. My anxiety level began to fall and I was put in Farley's cabin – a rare privilege, he reminded me. An hour later Feeney rolled me a smoke and I was able to ask some questions about what would happen next. I felt incredibly weary, but unable to sleep because of the numbing pain. I couldn't lie in one position for more than a few minutes before wanting to turn over.

At some point in the evening I heard the engine revs being eased as we approached the Broome port entrance. Orders were yelled and the mooring ropes were thrown.

I dragged myself up and onto the deck, then staggered off the boat to a car driven by Farley's partner, who took me to hospital. The medicos there prodded my neck and asked me about the bite. They seemed to think it was a box jellyfish, but there was none of the characteristic welts. Eventually they found a small rash under the side of my face.

They also detected a heart murmur that was the result of a massive whack of toxins into my nervous system. I would be stuck in hospital a while. Ramah was very upset, especially when the very next day, for a laugh, Norm and Shameless came up to my ward with pizzas and beer. She knew what was going on because her friend Amy Tang Wei worked as a nursing assistant, and kept her well informed. I tried the food and a sip of the beer, but I was still too far gone to be much fun. As I lay in bed reflecting on what had happened, I was grateful to Farley for taking me back into Broome so promptly. Delays during the neap cost the boat and crew money.

I knew also that I had been one of the lucky ones to have got a shot of pethidine. Most pearling boats carried nothing stronger than Panadol, although that would soon change. Mick Bray, who was such a tough bloke, had told me about the time he was stung; how he thought he would die of the pain.

'I told Badge, "You'd better tie me down because I think I'm going to do something stupid" [i.e., throw himself overboard]. I tried to describe the symptoms to him as they came on. There was intense pain, then a pause for a minute or two, and then it would come again, like someone was sticking a knife into you.'

THE LAST PEARLING LUGGER

The pain went on for twelve hours, Mick said, while the crew and then the doctors in Broome tried to work out what had happened. The Japanese divers thought it was the bends, while the medicos misdiagnosed it as a tentacle from a box jelly.

The lack of medical knowledge about the irukandji was one of the most frightening things. This particular jellyfish was first scientifically identified in 1964, but until the nineties it was little known and very poorly understood. Only an inch or so long and barely visible in the water, this obscure killer is made more dangerous by the stings it carries on its bell as well as its tentacles. Researchers now know that in fatalities, victims suffer from severe hypertension and die from bleeding in the brain: no wonder the pain is so intense! At least these days medical researchers are closer to developing an antivenene, and doctors are better trained to recognise the symptoms and prescribe an effective treatment.

* * *

BACK IN Broome, my heart gradually returned to its normal rhythm and I was released from hospital and cleared for diving again. I was told to keep out of big sessions at the Roey, a doctor's order that was not too hard to obey, given the way my body felt bruised and mangled, like I'd worn the worst of a few rounds with a heavyweight boxer.

I missed a neap, but then was back out there. It was an inauspicious season. We were steadily moving into deeper water of around sixty feet, fishing mostly live shell. The pickings were still scrappy. Farley's methodical drift patterns ensured that we all caught shell, but the return was not great as we explored for new shell patches. One of the problems was that the big cyclone which had buried Dick Morgan's pearl farm off Port Smith in 1980 had also covered many of the shallow beds we usually fished off the Three Sandhills and Wallal.

Our skipper was very anxious to find new ground and justify his investment in the new trawler but, being Farley, he was also methodical and disinclined to make panicky decisions. Eventually, too many lean neaps would force him to investigate another area southwest of Cape Bossut, a massive patch which we divers dubbed 'Compass Rose' because the coordinates overlapped the distinctive compass stamp on the standard Admiralty Charts of the day. Like most patches of pearl shell, it had been fished and recorded by an earlier generation of divers in the 1950s. There was not much coast along the Eighty Mile or north around the Lacepedes Islands that an earlier generation of Japanese had not investigated. The challenge for Farley would be how to safely dive in the deeper waters around that location.

Just to make things worse, there was a serious accident on the boat involving my mate Norm House, who had begun to work as a diver. Our air lines consisted of 60 metres of yellow hose linked to the compressor air filter on board. Norm always insisted on coiling his own air line at the end of the day and personally throwing it overboard next morning to ensure that there were no tangles.

His day got off to a bad start when a deckie heaved Norm's air line over as Farley set up the boat for a drift. Sure enough, there was a tangle shortly after. 'Half an hour into the drift, just when we had hit a stuffer patch, my air goes off,' Norm told me later.

'Raging free ascent from 70 feet – not fun. I abuse the deckie and sort out the hose. By then I had missed the drift. The rest of the divers came up with chocka bags and all I had was about half a dozen fucked old commies. Further abuse for the deckie and Farley.'

Farley was alternating dive teams, so Norm had to spend the next drift on deck waiting to haul up the divers' bags when they surfaced. For this purpose, Farley had installed overhead hydraulic winches which were bolted under the stern shelter deck. The capstan which controlled the winding of the winch was fastened to the deck's steel roof beams.

To operate the winch, you cranked down an overhead hydraulic lever to turn on the capstan, then looped a few coils of rope for the spinning winch drum to take up, and hauled in the shell bags which were attached to the other end of the rope. Occasionally the rope got tangled on the winch drum, as it did this day. When Norm tried to free the rope by reaching over the spinning capstan his arm was caught in the tangle. He was lifted bodily off the deck, in mortal danger of being fed through the winch like clothes through an old washing machine wringer.

I was working on the other side of the boat when I heard a hoarse scream and the crack of bone shattering. I turned around just in time to see Norm being jerked off his feet and about to be fed head first through the winch. Feeney was closer than I was, and managed to shut off the power. It was his shell bag, and he was quick out of the water to rescue Norm.

Larry took Norm's weight in a bear hug while Feeney reversed the capstan to free the mangled arm. The accident could have been much worse. Norm was wearing his wetsuit which we cut off, leaving the arm section to act as a splint. Blood was starting to seep through and there was an ugly distortion in his arm just below the elbow joint.

Fortunately, after my run-in with the irukandji, Farley had begun to carry pethidine on board. We stabilised Norm with a massive shot of it, and made him as comfortable as possible. Farley set course for La Grange Aboriginal community, radioing ahead for a four-wheel drive to be brought down to the beach. A dinghy was lowered and we drove Norm, now ashen-faced, ashore. We saw him into the vehicle before turning back to the boat. Poor old Norm was driven to the North West Coastal highway, where an ambulance met him, and then taken on to Broome Hospital, not arriving until ten hours after the accident.

The doctors at Broome sent him on to Derby for surgery – a botched job, as it turned out. Norm's diving career was over and he found himself and his newly riveted arm spending days propping up the bar at the Roebuck. Later X-rays showed that where there had been two breaks in his arm, there were now seven where the screws that were supposed to help mend the bone had been inserted.

It was bad news. Save for Medicare, there was no workers' compensation or any other financial support for Norm, except for wages for shell caught on his last diving trip. In 1981 in Western Australia, being a 'share fisherman' did not extend to payment for on-the-job injuries. His future did not look bright.

❋ ❋ ❋

THE LAST PEARLING LUGGER

NORM WASN'T my only old friend from art school days who had made his way up to the northwest. The third member of the Broome chapter of Caulfield Institute of Technology's Fine Art Department was Gary Proctor, who had arrived and found work with Norm's previous employer, Broome Pearls. Their boat *Pacific Lady* had a new skipper called Feathers. He was amiable, competent and easy-going, but his experience was on Gulf trawlers, not in pearling. Initially, the Lady had enjoyed several successful neaps and after some encouragement from Proctor that the good times would keep on rolling, I thought about the lean, mean season we were experiencing on Farley's trawler, and for better or worse decided to switch ships.

In anticipation of an improvement to my bank account I signed on to the old scow mid-season, but what a mistake that was. A few weeks later Farley finally moved into the deep water and hit a stuffer patch lying in 120 feet of water on the fabled Compass Rose. My new assignment was not all it was cracked up to be, as I soon found out. There were a few days when we actually managed a respectable tally of shell, but my recollections are of a dysfunctional boat. The Lady had seen better days, and breakdowns were a regular feature of trips to the grounds. Downtime for repairs meant that as share fishermen we were not earning, but paying out on food and fuel.

One neap, the gearbox blew up and we had to be towed back to Broome by George King's wooden trawler, the *Easterley*. Soon after that incident, Feathers had to put out a 'Pan Pan' call – only one grade lower than an SOS – because the engine seized when we were adrift on the high seas.

On another occasion, we ran out of drinking water, something that should never have happened. When we radioed for a fresh supply to be brought down, some shore-based drongo back in Broome filled half a dozen new steel jerry cans for us. When they were brought down on a supply run the water was found to be undrinkable, contaminated by an oily rust retardant coating the inside of the container.

In desperation the German cook, Detlef, whose meals were so bad that we had threatened to feed him to the sharks, improvised a distillation device using metres of copper pipe that we kept on board for emergencies. In the process of extracting enough water for a cup of coffee, he used up the best part of an entire gas cylinder. That was the end of him.

Then, as we floundered our way around the Eighty Mile, Proctor was stung by a dream fish, that tiny fish that likes to live in the heel of old pearl shell, and injects a walloping dose of toxin into any unwelcome gloved hand that comes its way. Poor old Gary was out of the water for the rest of the day on a diet of painkillers, until eventually his hand shrank back to normal after swelling up to the size of a baseball mitt.

Surely pearling was never meant to be like this, I thought to myself. One day, when I was just about at the end of my tether, we closed on the *DMcD*, now skippered by Big Bag. Feathers, who monitored the radio and watched what the other boats were doing, thought that the old lugger appeared to be making a good catch, so we set up our own drift nearby.

I was diving on an outside line, and underwater could just make out Shameless in the distant. I swam over to him, indicated I wanted to swap diving gear, unhitched my reg and weight belt – and then surfaced to some surprised faces on the *DMcD*. Shane's appearance on the *Pacific Lady* met an equally stunned reception. I stayed overnight exchanging gossip with my old mates Big Bag and Squire before returning next day. That short spell on the *DMcD* was enough to convince me that I was not long for the Lady.

One of the stories we sat around discussing concerned the *Beacon K*, Broome Pearls' predecessor to the *Pacific Lady*. Predictably enough, the company's decision to fish commercial shell through the wet season of 1979–80 had got off to a bumpy start. Somewhere off La Grange, the torque converter in the 25-metre trawler seized, leaving the *Beacon K* without any propulsion or auxiliary power.

The crew included the principals of Broome Pearls, John Foxlow and Ian Turner, as well as Russell Massey, Bazza Thorpe, Shameless Shane Ford, Ian Fanny, Peter 'Flex' Lake and Lindsay Brady. Foxlow and Turner went off to get help by catching a dinghy ride to shore and then walking across country for about ten kilometres through the bush near La Grange Mission onto the North West Coastal highway. There they would hitch a lift back to Broome.

Over the next four days, the crew left marooned on the steel trawler under the baking tropical sun went a little stir crazy. The food in the freezers started to go off, inspiring a food fight that lasted three days. 'There were tubs of margarine splattered all through the wheelhouse. It was feral, like something out of *Lord of the Flies*,' Shameless recalled later.

If food stocks were in peril then at least the boat held an adequate supply of alcohol. No one used that as a missile. To kill time over drinks the crew fished for shark. Whole chickens and lumps of prime cube roll from the freezer were fastened onto heavy duty hooks connected by mooring ropes to the mast by a series of pulleys. Empty fuel drums were used as a float.

As the freezer contents were progressively emptied overboard, the water became heavily berleyed. The fishermen did not have to wait too long for a shark. Altogether, nine were caught, including a monster tiger. The water was so clear that night that Shameless remembers seeing the sharks take the bait lit up by phosphorescence.

Once the sharks' jaw bones were stripped and the fins cut away, the crew hoisted the carcasses into the rigging by the tails, macabre talismans.

On the day they were rescued, Shameless and his mates decided to put on a special welcome for the two engineers flown up from Perth to fix the ship's propulsion system. They climbed the rigging and wheelhouse and hopped about like monkeys whooping and swinging off ropes. The engineers apparently gazed in wide-eyed amazement at this ship festooned with rotting sharks and crewed by demented pearlers. Discipline was always a bit of a problem on the boats run by Broome Pearls.

* * *

ONE INCIDENT in particular drove my decision to leave the *Pacific Lady*.

THE LAST PEARLING LUGGER

The morning had been quite choppy, one of those days with a blustery sou'easter blowing off the land and the boat rolling in the swells so hard that stepping off the diver's ladder into the deep blue was like that blissful release you get when a hangover finally stops hammering at your temples.

We were working in quite deep water – about twenty-five metres – and visibility was clear as it usually was on the first dive of the morning. For once, there was a bit of shell lying around, prompting a keen contest among the divers to fill their work bags. Without warning, the air in my hose started to run out. I jerked the yellow line a few times hoping to clear what I thought was a kink in it caused by the choppy conditions up top. This solved the problem, so I resumed my search for shell. The drift ended and we surfaced, the water still clear enough for me to look across at the other three divers. We had all caught a reasonable tally of pearl shell.

After a quick cup of tea, snacks and – for the tobacco addicts among the divers – a smoke, it was back into the water. Feathers lined up on the buoy marking the shell patch and we got our gear on for another drift. The deckie hoisted the drogue overboard and the old trawler slowed down to a virtual stall as we piled overboard.

I had only been on the bottom for a few minutes when the air went off again. I turned around and again yanked the hose; again the air came back on. About fifteen minutes later I had a neck bag that was almost full of shell when the air started to run out for a third time.

I wasn't worried, and continued to swim out to pick up a couple more shell, the sudden burst of energy causing me to breathe harder. I jerked the hose – but this time no air followed.

I released the work line and began to drift to the surface automatically, my only connection to the boat now the air line. As the seconds ticked by I started to worry how long it would take me to reach the surface. I ditched my neck bag, watching it tumble to the bottom in a plume of sandy dust as it settled. Next, I unclipped my weight belt to relieve the drag, which meant I was no longer connected to my air line as I desperately tried to get topside.

The rippling blue surface was tantalisingly close. My stomach began to palpitate and I urinated involuntarily as I kicked frantically for the surface, expelling what little compressed air I had last inhaled to avoid an embolism. Nearly on the point of blacking out, I punched the surface, sucking in a mix of seawater and fresh air. Coughing violently, I started swimming for the boat. I was totally knackered but at least I was alive.

On deck an argument ensued between me and the head diver. He claimed my hose was old and prone to kinking, but I was unconvinced. I suspected his deckie mate had been 'playing' with my hose as a distraction to put me off catching shell. It was an old trick, to temporarily turn off the air by squeezing off the hose and then releasing it again.

That night in the galley, serious words were exchanged about the safety of the gear. My air was never cut off again but I was finished with the *Pacific Lady*.

Weeks later, after a wild springs celebration in town, the entire *Pacific Lady* crew were arrested and carted off to the Broome lock-up for the night. I had narrowly escaped the police round-up and, feeling a bit guilty, ran an errand to the local fast food joint to bring back Chiko rolls and gaspers. I was able to gain access to the lock-up, situated at the rear of the police station, by scaling a large frangipani tree by the side of the building. The roof of the detention cells were open air and secured with wire mesh so I was able to pass down the care packages.

* * *

BACK ONSHORE, I found that Norm's trials had continued.

On the advice of the local magistrate, of all people, he tried for compo from Roebuck Deep Pearls. Farley replied with a legal opinion, and without the money to contest his case Norm folded after accepting a token payout.

Evidence tendered by skipper Alan Nunn, a friend of Farley, helped scupper Norm's compo bid. It showed that while fishing technology had advanced, fairness and equity for workers in the pearling industry had not. 'Nunny gave evidence that I had worked with Billy Hart removing a tree from his backyard while my arm was still in a cast. Fuck, it was Bill's way of helping a mate in trouble with some acceptable charity work and for those wealthy pearling masters to seize on that – I thought was an all time low act,' Norm told me.

His diving days were over. Yet he remained in Broome a while longer with his girlfriend, Karen, who was able to get work at the local hospital while Norm's arm recovered. Eventually he landed some casual work, including a short driving stint with his old mate Ted Foster hauling water in the old Mack truck for road gangs working the black soil country out on Roebuck Plains.

CHAPTER 13

Introducing 'Dad'

As hellish as season '81 had been, I was not yet finished with pearl fishing. The following year, come March, I signed up with another member of the PPL fleet, the B-6. After my peremptory dismissal by Badger, I considered myself lucky to be asked back by PPL. In 1982, the rates that the company paid contract divers were among the best: $3 for each 'live' shell caught, a tidy sum in those days. By contrast divers working in deep water with Bruce Farley earnt $1 per live shell and about 75 cents a commie.

Many divers, myself included, also felt it was safer working with PPL because the fleet luggers predominantly fished only shallow water to depths of around 20 metres.

In contrast, Farley often worked the deep water, and deep water meant more risk of the bends.

The downside of the B-6, as I would soon discover, was its skipper, Alan Nunn, known as 'Dad'. Onshore he was a prominent member of the local tennis club and the reigning Broome men's singles champ. On the boats he cultivated a tough guy image. We all heard stories of how his early days in Broome were filled with wild drinking sprees onshore, a bit like the mob I went around with.

There was no doubt that PPL had been well served by Dad. A trained boilermaker, he had put his welding skills to good use in the design of steel outriggers when the last of the luggers was converted to hookah operation. His diving prowess was unquestioned and his shell tallies credible.

But strange things can happen to a man's mind after years at sea. Niggling inadequacies become magnified, and perhaps this was the case with Dad. Once he and Badger had been close friends, but now there was intense rivalry between them. It was a contest each neap to see who could take most shell, and almost invariably Badger won, an outcome that merely spurred the moody B-6 lugger skipper into deeper and darker moods.

He liked his crew to call him 'Dad' and even had this moniker penned in black marker ink on his regulation orange plastic coffee mug, as if we might forget. I never got the meaning, because he was anything but fatherly to me. The pre-season fit out was a taste of the ordeal ahead.

To be fair, Dad had reason to be narky at the start of the season. During the lay-off he had sought to make some improvements to his Broome abode, and called for quotes to brick in extra living space on the ground floor. Bazza

THE LAST PEARLING LUGGER

Thorpe and Shameless Shane's wet season lifestyle meant they were in need of cash. They gave the lowest quote and scored the job. A building contract which should have been completed in a matter of weeks was stretched into months. Magic mushroom season proved something of a distraction. And huge bills for cement were run up because at four o'clock each day the boys downed tools to head to the Roey, tipping wheelbarrows of fresh mixed cement into an adjacent vacant block.

The ploy worked for a while until a grass fire swept the block, revealing their wastage and causing Dad to have a Category One meltdown. In response, the bricklayers showed up for work dressed in suits purchased at the local op shop. Dad sensed this gesture toward responsibility was completely ironic. At that point he gave up on them. That is not to say either were unskilled tradies. Weeks earlier, the pair had hauled a massive slab of sandstone from Gantheaume Point back to Carol's house where they laboriously and meticulously carved a compass rose complete with all the cardinal points – a variation on the whaler's scrimshaw of old.

The B-6 was a grand old dame of the fleet with a beam that suggested her builders had an aircraft carrier deck in mind when they laid the keel. She was one plank higher and two planks wider than the rest of the PPL boats. On lugger maintenance, Dad was a perfectionist and not a dollar was spared (well, it wasn't his money). He was obsessed with stainless steel (after all, he hailed from Newcastle), and insisted on stainless fastenings on every fixture on the lugger. He was also just as obsessed as Farley had been with keeping the steel shell tanks clean. Jif parties, as we all called them, were a regular feature of lugger life for all the crew.

Early each morning you could find us on the B-6 at her mooring off Streeters Jetty, crawling around on deck on our hands and knees scrubbing rust off steel stanchions, exposed nuts and bolts, wherever iron oxide was in evidence. The lugger's big steel shell tank was scrubbed so clean you could have eaten from it. It was a shame the same conditions were not adhered to on PPL's two mother ships, which in contrast to the luggers were floating germ labs, and the cause of future high shell mortality.

One day another diver and I were given the job of melting lead ingots with an oxy torch and pouring the molten mix into steel water pipe, to be cast as down weights for divers. It was a tricky job, because molten lead has a tendency to blow back and burn you. There were no masks, no leather gloves, and no overalls. This was dangerous work done in the open, while we were attired in nothing more than tee-shirts, footy shorts and thongs.

Unlike Badger's B-3 which had been stripped of its sails, the B-6 came fully gaff-rigged, so our pre-season fit out also included fixing newly refurbished Oregon spars with sail cloth and rigging the block and tackle used to hoist the sails. All Dad's crew were required to help in fitting out the lugger and ensuring the boat was spic and span for the start of the season. There were a few recruits from Farley's boat who had gained experience working several seasons in deep water, including Wonder Pup, Wayne House's younger brother Larry. As well there was Steve Oats, an experienced diver who had formerly worked for Paspaley, and John Battersby, an immensely likeable kid from Newcastle who was not even out of his teens.

The Bat, as we dubbed him, was super fit, a black belt in karate. Though he was a newcomer, in the medical exam for our divers' licence that year he had been declared the fittest candidate, the nurses revealing his pulse hardly altered after the cardiopulmonary test. He seemed unstoppable, as the story of his memorable maiden trip to Broome attested. He had driven up alone from Perth in his burnt orange Holden ute, a journey that was long but uneventful until his car collected an emu one evening. He was travelling at speed when the big bird hit, caving in his windscreen. With a bloody feathered carcass sitting in his lap as tried to steer the car, he narrowly avoided a rollover. I saw his ute later – it looked like it had been driven into a brick wall. Totalling motor vehicles became something of a rite of passage for pearl divers returning for the start of a new season.

The previous year Zimmo had written off his fire engine west of the Isa by Evel Knievelling into a creek bed after missing a bridge late one night.

One morning on the boat I found Johnny the Bat in the galley, shovelling down a bowl of breakfast cereal without any milk or even fruit juice – just grinding up the dry husks and none too happy about it. He was acting literally on Dad's advice to divers that a dairy-free breakfast was the way to avoid the mucous-linked ear blockages that they tended to suffer. I told the Bat that constipation was the only certain outcome, and suggested that he try using skim milk in future.

Before the fleet put to sea, the pearling season was formally opened with the traditional lugger picnic which included a race across Roebuck Bay. When sprigs of mangrove were tied to the top of the mast for good luck, I could only reflect that Dad would need it. His great rival, Badger's B-3, no longer had sails, so it acted as the official start and finish line. But the race was usually won by a sleek, narrow-hulled Japanese lugger, the B-1, and this year was no exception if memory serves me.

Although the *DMcD* usually gave the B-1 a run for her money, any notion this was a classic yacht race should be laid to rest. Under sail, luggers performed sluggishly even if assisted by gusting winds slicing across the bay. None of the fleet was more sluggish than Dad's B-6, which on one celebrated occasion a few years before had crossed the finish line stern first. I was on board the *DMcD* that time, and the best I could do was hold my ribs to stop the pain from laughing too hard as Big Bag, who was monitoring proceedings with his binoculars, offered up a race commentary.

Dad had ordered his tipsy guests to pack onto the forward deck in order to correct the wayward direction of his lugger. But, rather like the proverbial shuffling of deckchairs on the *Titanic*, this command proved ineffectual. As the broad backside of the B-6 eased across the finish line to hoots and jeers from amused onlookers, Dad's reputation suffered another unjust blow.

Dad enjoyed the power that came with being a lugger skipper. At the start of one neap when the weather was particularly rough he ordered the divers to swim out to the lugger anchored more than a kilometre away in the channel. It was dawn when we gathered at Town Beach, and mackerel skies pointed to an overcast day ahead.

THE LAST PEARLING LUGGER

A gusty sou'-wester blowing in from the sea was throwing up big swells and white caps. The water was chilly, but we obeyed orders and began swimming out toward the lugger.

The tide was running strong, as it so often did around Broome. Large waves picked us up and flung us back like flotsam as we tried to cross the surf line, laughing at first but then cursing the exhausting folly of the order. Eventually, a dinghy set off from the lugger to collect us. I clearly remember the dark shape of the boat looming over the top of a huge wave as I swam frantically to get clear before it could crash down on me.

The rest of the fleet was halfway down to the grounds by the time we clambered onto the B-6, totally knackered and wondering what crazy idea Dad would come up with next.

Not all of his ideas were wacky. He liked to have a lot of fish in the freezer – a big plus – so we often stopped off at False Cape Bossut on the way down to the grounds for a swim and the chance to spear some reef fish, coral trout, blue bone or cod. He was insanely competitive. His constant rantings about his spear fishing prowess required an answer. At the end of one neap, for a lark I challenged him that my hand lines could catch more fish than he could spear. Sure enough, he took the bet that I offered him for a keg of beer and we went to work.

I set up four hand lines on each side of the deck tied off on the wire overhead stays. In a few minutes I had bites and began hauling in an impressive mix of reef fish. Dad surfaced once with a fish on the end of his spear. Seeing my catch, he immediately ordered the other divers in to assist. Now I was competing with four other spear fishermen.

I kept pulling in fish but with his extra help Dad quickly amassed a big pile to be judged on weight by the head diver – a fair weather ally. I was naturally biased and thought I had the biggest haul. But the arbitrator, Dave Jackson, gave it to Dad and the cost of a keg was duly docked from my pay.

Our next challenge came when I decided to take Dad on at tennis. I had not picked up a racket in years but I got a buzz throwing down the gauntlet, because I could see it rattled him. He eagerly grabbed the challenge, soundly beating me before a crowd of bemused spectators at Broome Tennis Club. At least I managed to blast a few sizzling aces around his feet.

I offered up the keg as promised but his wife declined. 'I hope you're not thinking of having that at our place,' she said. My friends and I drained it ourselves, joking about the match. Dad was invited, but chose not to share a drink with the crew. True to form, he docked another barrel from my next wages.

At the start of the season we began fishing in close, diving on the legendary potato country off Mangrove Point. It was legendary because it seldom failed to produce a bountiful harvest of young pearl shell each year. But the key to a good haul was having a keen eye to identify the shell, which was disguised with great clods of marine growth which was the result of the better light.

I was only an average diver in potato country. The others, especially Oats and Larry, managed repeated big hauls of shell. But once we moved further south into deeper clearer water my tally began to rise and with it the prospects of a healthy pay packet at the end of the neap. By now Dad obviously thought of me as a bit of a shit stirrer, but I was able to keep my job at least until he could find a suitable replacement.

Dad had been vexed about divers being too slow to get into the water after he set up for a drift. So we began diving in before the drogue was set, prompting grumbles about going in too soon. One morning, fully rigged for a dive, I was first to jump off the ladder. The next thing I knew, Dad had pulled the drogue and opened the throttle, yelling at me for entering the water too soon.

Obviously in a temper, he took me for a tow, gunning the motor and pulling me along behind the boat by my air hose. The force of the water nearly tore my face mask off. I got a brief glimpse of several crew standing on the stern looking on stunned. It was a reckless act that could easily have resulted in my drowning if I had become tangled in the gear.

When Dad slowed to let me aboard I gave him a huge scrve, just resisting a growing desire to punch his lights out. I'm sure he felt the same about me. Angry words were exchanged down the deck before we both went into neutral corners on the boat but I was furious.

The pent-up anger exploded below decks later that evening when he started up again, standing on the focsle ladder bellowing abuse at me below. I remember Oats grabbing my arm to prevent me from getting up and hauling him off the steps. It was probably a good move.

* * *

Back on shore, totally uninvited, Dad came early one morning into the digs where Ramah and I were now living – a state-owned house shared with our friend Mindau, a dental assistant. He had heard all the rumours about our wild parties and I suspect the visit had been planned for some time. We'd been partying hard the night before and bodies and detritus were strewn everywhere on the morning of his house call, half naked bodies flaked on the couch, bongs, overflowing ashtrays, empty beer bottles. Normally the house was kept clean and tidy; on this occasion it definitely was not.

I found myself rudely jolted from slumber as Dad suddenly poked his rough head into my bedroom. Sneering, he shouted a demand to get down to the jetty for a work detail. He had decided at short notice to call a work party to anti-foul the lugger hull. There was no warning of his arrival. Another crewman off our boat was crashed out in an adjacent bedroom with a new-found friend, quaking in fear that the boss would burst in after waking me.

This was the final straw for me in my relationship with Dad. Home invasion was overstepping the mark. I suspected there was more to it than just an announcement for an unscheduled work party – he wanted to see how we lived and reckoned that, given I was living in state housing leased by an indigenous tenant, he would probably get away with his uninvited intrusion.

My crewmates and I assembled to sweat out our hangovers in the sandfly-infested swamp beside Streeters Jetty. Walshy tried to raise our spirits with a falsetto rendition of a Cliff Richard song playing on his walkman. Although I saw out the day's work, I decided that I had had enough of

Dad and his bizarre antics and angry demands. The money was good but not enough of an inducement for me to want to stay and work for him.

The music continued to blare even when there was nobody on deck, when Big Bag was below tinkering in the engine room or cooking up a scoff in the galley, and the divers were all on the bottom.

I walked soon after, and followed up my resignation with an angry letter to PPL's managing director, Alec Myer, complaining about the way in which skippers like Dad were able to operate. It was one of the first official complaints that were made about the arbitrary conduct of some lugger captains, and although I was unaware of it at the time, my letter had repercussions when Dad was later questioned over it by PPL management.

My last act after cleaning out my stuff and leaving the boat was to dump some rubbish in an incinerator at the end of Streeters Jetty. The box was filled with old rags and waste paper, engine room detritus and a near empty can of aero-start, a volatile spray which was blasted into the air intake to coax stubborn old diesel engines into life.

No sooner had I dropped the box into the drum and walked a couple of paces when there was a massive explosion and a huge fireball of smoke in the perfect shape of a mushroom cloud, an appropriate ending, I felt.

I had managed to save a few dollars so my finances were not parlous. My position was quickly taken by another recent arrival in Broome, John Kelly, who was fresh off the Gulf prawn trawlers and keen to get a start on the luggers. An asthma sufferer, he kept quiet about the condition and got past his diving medicals. Over subsequent months, we became good friends with a shared loathing of Dad. At the end of the season, Kel also quit the B-6.

It was eight weeks before I signed onto another lugger – the venerable old *DMcD*. I was hired as watch-keeper/diver and began work on October 1, the back end of the 1982 season.

The crew consisted of the skipper Big Bag, Squire, his business partner, and Feeney and Shameless. There was also Cossack, a Thursday Islander, Perry, a former member of the British Paratroop Regiment who had seen active service in Northern Ireland, and Hard Porn Holmes, a bikie turned diver. It was like coming home to be among so many familiar faces.

CHAPTER 14

Back to the *DMcD*

The *DMcD* was a generally happy ship, crewed by the most genial mob of desperadoes this side of the 26th parallel. We included the cream of PPL's rejects, which was to us a badge of honour. To celebrate our notoriety we took to flying a massive pirate flag from the mast.

Perhaps to complete the look, Shameless Shane took to fastening mackerel lures to his ears as a form of adornment. When Zimmo stepped off the flash *Paspaley I* onto the *DMcD*, Shameless greeted him with his usual menacing refrain – 'You're not on Daddy's yacht any more'. This became our mantra whenever visitors arrived. While the wages were lower than the going rates on other boats we were by far the happiest crew, working under minimum management under the nominal command of the ever unflappable Big Bag. There were languid summer days when we had set up our drift, sea dead calm, divers on the bottom and Big Bag in the galley or engine room checking oil or cleaning air filters.

Like the fabled *Mary Celeste* there was no visible sign of life on deck apart from the steady, repetitive chug of diesel engine and the strains of Roxy Music's *Avalon* wafting across the water from our onboard stereo. To my mind this was the last pearling lugger.

Using proceeds from the sale of pearl shell meat, Shameless bought two large speakers for the boat. He rigged them to the mast and wired them into a cassette player. All day while we worked, we played our music loud. Richard Clapton's 'Capricorn Dancer' got a lot of air play that summer. Other favourites ranged from The Angels to Grace Jones's *Warm Leatherette* and the escapist fantasy of Ozark Mountain Daredevils' *The Car over the Lake Album* (a Shameless perennial – he may have been the group's greatest fan). When Squire came out on deck, the music took on a distinct country flavour.

The *DMcD*'s journey had been interesting to say the least since Big Bag and Squire acquired the old lugger from Farley back at the end of the 1979 season, and christened their venture Barrow Pearls. After heading off some local opposition at Onslow, Steve and Big Bag were granted a pearl lease and fishing quota there. Onslow had had its moment of fame (or infamy) in the 1950s, when it served as a base for British atomic tests in the Monte Bello islands. Squire found a massive pair of pearl shell there; double the size of anything I ever saw in Broome, and cause for speculation that they were some kind of atomic mutant.

The boys began by fishing at Giralia Bay, deep in the mouth of Exmouth Gulf. It was not a comfortable place to be in mid-January. That first month of 1980, temperatures soared into the forties, as the cloying humidity of the wet season combined with baking heat off the adjacent desert during the day. So the *DMcD* headed back closer to the ocean coast, temporarily mooring at Learmonth.

Big Bag went to Fremantle with another Farley veteran Mark Feeney who had offered his skippering services. They would study for their Master 5 skipper's tickets under the redoubtable Captain Jardine. In Freo, they ran into John Stewart, their old crewmate, who had signed up for the same course. It was a fateful meeting with the Colonel.

Over beers at the Esplanade Hotel John agreed to rent his six-metre work boat to his friends. The plan was for Big Bag to sit his exams and return to Onslow with the necessary qualifications to skipper the *DMcD*, which was still registered as a commercial fishing boat. In the interim, Squire would run the Colonel's Star boat to fish for shell. A skipper's ticket was not needed for the smaller craft, a large aluminium fishing boat with outboard motors, and mother-of-pearl could still be sold by the drum for cash to brokers like Perth-based Jack Krasenstein in order to raise some much needed capital at the start of the pearling season.

On his way up from Perth Wonder Dog dropped in for a week or so to see the boys and lend a diving hand. A backpacker had been recruited to drive the Star boat, a bloke called Andy, another denizen of the Palace who had just returned from a second Kimberley expedition with my old travelling companion, Al Burton. Andy was light on for pearl fishing experience, so he was given the job of driving the boat and tendering while Squire, Walshy and Wonder dived for shell.

The days were long and hard drifting deep inside the gulf around Roberts Island. Once they had found their shell and landed it, it had to be cleaned and packed into hessian bags all within the confines of a tiny sixteen-footer. Nevertheless at first everything went well. The water in Giralia Bay is not all that deep – only around thirteen metres. As the fishing went on, the Colonel's little craft began to fill with bags of shell which were stacked in the forward compartment.

One day, close to 4 pm, Walshy was busy picking up shell on the sea bottom when he felt his air supply getting thin. An experienced diver, he turned to check his hose for kinks but nothing prepared him for the sight that was about to greet him. On his way up to the surface, he passed the air compressor heading down, followed by the Colonel's Star boat itself.

While the two divers had been busy collecting shell back up top on the surface Andy had been chopping, cleaning and packing pearl shell. However, he had inadvertently stacked most of the bags on the port side, resulting in a steadily increasing list.

As the heavily laden boat continued its awkward drift through choppy sea, water began to pour through the scuppers flooding the stern under the floorboards. By the time Andy realised his predicament, it was too late. He tried to gun the engine and get the boat up on a plane to right the worsening list but she was too far gone. The engine stalled and the vessel quickly sank by the stern.

The water was warm and, after gathering a few useful items floating on the surface, the trio began swimming for their lives to the nearest landfall, Roberts Island, about three kilometres away. The two experienced divers took turns to drag Andy, who was a much poorer swimmer, behind them. It was the first of several exhausting swims.

Walshy recalled afterwards that he had to ditch most of his diving gear in order to keep going. 'I think except for my jocks I was starkers.' They made it safely to Roberts Island, but Andy was unable to complete the next leg, a long haul across the tide to the mainland somewhere off Exmouth Station, a location only approximately fixed by sighting the gleaming radio towers of a distant defence installation.

Darkness was falling, and the temperature was dropping, so they dug themselves into the sand and huddled together. After a freezing night the two divers decided to head for shore to get help. Andy would be left marooned on the island until they returned with help. The pair decided to try and reach the station using the distant radio masts as a reference. The mainland was still about four or five kilometres distant, but at least they had a flipper each.

'After a few hours we came ashore, I think a couple of kilometres short of where we had been aiming for. By that stage, we'd had no food or water for more than twenty-four hours.' They had just crossed a stretch of water that was one of the most shark-infested anywhere along the Australian coastline, a fact which they only learnt later.

Steve and Walshy tried to remember where they had last seen the radio towers. Badly heat affected and dehydrated they stumbled off into the scrub following a fence line they hoped would lead them to the station. 'We were thinking we had better get a move on. We were both totally sunburnt. It was so bad I'd taken my jocks off and put them on my head. I was starkers walking through the bush in the nude,' Walshy told me. He thought it was the fact that they were both still young men that got them through. 'After a couple more hours I began thinking, *we're going to die if we're not careful, if we don't find the station soon.*'

They had made a wrong turn, which took them four kilometres out of their way. Walshy became delirious with sunstroke, and somewhere near the station he collapsed into a sheep trough. Steve kept walking and made it to the homestead around 3 pm.

The family living there were amazed when Squire, half naked and semi-delirious, staggered in seeking help. They provided first aid and arranged to have the pair taken to Exmouth Hospital for a check-up. In their delirium, the divers almost forgot about Andy, left behind on the island.

Not that others had any trouble locating him. He had managed to dry some matches and had set fire to the undergrowth as a signal. Unfortunately, the blaze quickly developed into a spectacular bushfire that engulfed the entire island. George King, a local prawn trawler operator, rescued Andy who was by then suffering extreme dehydration, a condition aggravated by his scavenging for oysters and a near incineration after the bushfire. He had been on the island for two nights with nothing to drink, and only a feed of oysters from the rocks.

There was little time for the crew to recover from the sinking before they went back to work to salvage the wreck. Steve brought the lugger down to search for the boat, which was located after the bright yellow air hoses were spotted floating in a tangled mess on the surface. 'We spent another day getting the boat up again. Finally when it was floating we started a tow back to Exmouth. Then we lost the tow and it sank again. By this time when we get it up, it's all buckled and twisted,' said Walshy.

It was an inauspicious start to the Barrow Pearls venture, but at least the Colonel, as amiable as ever, took the sinking in his stride. No doubt the blow was softened by the generous compensation payment he received from Big Bag.

* * *

ALTHOUGH THEY'D eventually made a go of things at Onslow, Steve and Big Bag had always wanted to return to Broome. In 1981 they turned the *DMcD* north, and leased a pearl farm at Beagle Bay, a picturesque safe haven for luggers about 120 kilometres north of Broome. At the time it seemed like a workable arrangement. Big Bag looked after the fishing and Steve ran the day to day business dealings while investigating pearl seeding techniques.

Despite their practical skills and love of the sea, the pair were completely different personalities. Steve was a thinker and dreamer, attracted to technology and innovation. By

1982 home computers had just started to come on the market. I had no idea what they were and, like most of the crew, regarded them with some suspicion especially after Steve began tightening up Barrow Pearl's informal approach to bookkeeping. For us the future began with PayDive, the world's first computerised payslip for pearl divers.

Unfortunately, Steve treated his PC much as he did his diving gear. I remember him heaving his screen, computer and printer onto the front seat of the Land Cruiser just the same way that you would a healthy young dog, then driving the bone-jolting journey along a rough bush track that led to the Beagle Bay pearl farm. There, Steve would spend weeks and months in virtual solitary confinement trying to divine the puzzle of the cultured pearl, and patiently recording his results.

In contrast, Big Bag was a traditionalist and a man of action, despite his facility as a yarnspinner and mastery of the droll one-liner. Office work and record keeping were dark arts to him. Bruce was at ease tinkering away in the cramped engine room on the lugger or trying to discover the ultimate fix for our signal hose, which was forever faulty. The more time I spent with him, the more I realised how the ten years that he had spent shearing had marked him. In that tough world, you learnt to do things properly, economically and efficiently. Often, initially, you had to improvise. But ingenious improvisation gradually became tried and true ways, the basis of a routine that you stuck with until you wore it out. Change for change's sake was not a good thing.

CHAPTER 15

Dabbling in new waters

Ever since I had stepped off the B-6, I had begun to focus on the question that eventually confronts all pearl divers who are not killed by the job – how much longer?

I felt deeply torn. The pearlers from the 'class of '79' were a pretty unique mob. Rather like old Vietnam vets, whatever our personal and political differences we had formed a lasting bond during our years on the luggers. Yet for some of my friends pearling had already lost its allure, and they were looking for the exits. Norm packed his bags at the end of 1982. Karen was pregnant, so the couple decided to make a new life in rural Victoria. Shameless spray-painted an unsolicited black GT stripe over their car as a parting gesture.

'Doddy, you've been doing this gig four years. How long are you planning to stay an aqua-man?' Norm asked me before he headed out of town.

I could understand why Norm felt ready to leave after his attempts to obtain workers' compensation were snuffed out by the pearling bosses. The system did not favour workers, and the situation was not helped by the differing agendas of the divers, many of whom were utter mavericks dedicated to their narrow specialisation. Diving was their only chosen work, and involvement in litigation might well prejudice their already limited employment prospects.

My mate Bazza Thorpe was also facing a challenging future for fitness reasons. Both he and his partner, Carol, a cook-deckie, were working for Paspaley when Bazz was diagnosed with bone necrosis. A strong diver and keen sportsman, he had been complaining for weeks that his shoulder hurt. A Perth specialist confirmed the worst.

Avascular necrosis is an occupational hazard for commercial divers. It occurs when there is temporary or even permanent loss of blood supply to the bones, and the bone tissue dies causing the bone to collapse. Medical researchers believe that diving causes the blood vessels to narrow. In Bazza's case, his shoulder joint was affected. Often to relieve the pain, he would swing his arm and you could hear the clicking of the degraded joint.

Bazza received his prognosis during Shinju Matsuri, the traditional annual Japanese festival of the pearl. At the festival ball that night, he had a good glow up when he spotted the town's resident medico, Doctor Reid, seated at a nearby table. A powerfully built young man, Bazz advanced menacingly toward the doctor before bursting into song in parody of the band. 'Doctor, doctor, give me the news – I've got a bad case of the bone necrosis blues.' A relieved Doc Reid breathed out.

Yet though he made light of it, the news was a heavy blow for Bazza, who lived an active life outdoors and hated cities. Carol would later confide that it brought their relationship to a complete standstill.

Around the same time, I split up with Ramah. It came as a surprise to many of our friends, but the break-up had been building for months. Broome was her home, but after five years on the boats I was getting itchy feet. We had reached a point where our lives were diverging. It wasn't that I was missing Melbourne. It had become clear to me that I wanted to move on from diving, which would mean my eventual departure from Broome. I wanted a clean break. My decision did not make for an easy separation. Ramah and I spent a boozy evening sitting on the warm rocks at Gantheaume Point to talk things through; it ended in tears.

For years, I had dabbled in journalism's shallows, thinking that one day I would go in deeper. Now in my late twenties, I was starting to feel some self-imposed deadline approaching.

Before signing onto the luggers, I had worked as a volunteer journo for a local newsletter, the *Broome News*, published by an American named Kevin Lawton who was keen to establish a reputation as a short-story writer. Each week he penned a new chapter in the fictional life of a young man from Melbourne recently arrived in Broome. I drew cartoons and wrote urban affairs and town planning stories for the paper, including observations of indigenous life on Kennedy Hill, the Aboriginal community perched on prime real estate overlooking Dampier Creek and Roebuck Bay. Judging by the size of the midden pile there, it could probably qualify as one of the longest continuing human settlements in Australia, but in the early eighties the community was a ramshackle collection of pindan-stained besser block and tin shacks, set on a sunbaked sand dune straddling an ancient pyramid of oyster shells and broken glass. Taking a leaf out of Orwell, I tried – clumsily, I suppose – to convey the desolate inadequacy of the conditions there.

My first amateurish attempts at writing for a major magazine began while I was diving on the *DMcD* at the end of the '82 season. I penned a few columns about deep-water pearl fishing for an industry publication, *Professional Fisherman*, and attached a colour photograph that I had taken of Shameless and Cossack using a block and tackle to haul up a work bag stuffed with pearl shell. To get the shot I clambered out on the end of the outrigger, and the result was quite a dramatic photograph. I was pleasantly surprised when it landed on the cover and Shameless and Cossack became fishing legends. This success was enough to encourage me.

Meanwhile my itchy feet took me overseas during the 1982 lay-up. I went to Thailand, with the intention of again visiting Burma, a country which had a small but thriving pearling industry centred on the Mergui Archipelago. Before I left, I obtained a letter of introduction from Steve Arrow. It was typewritten by his girlfriend on tissue thin paper, with no letterhead and mistakes painted out with correction fluid. The Australian Embassy's trade commission in Bangkok kindly retyped the letter, in which Steve sought Burmese government assistance to allow tenured pearl technicians to come to Australia to advise on round pearl cultivation. This was a big ask.

In 1982 the technique to 'seed' round pearls was still a closely guarded secret of the highly paid Japanese operators who were flown in by Australian pearling companies. Almost every one in the Broome industry wanted to unravel the mystery. There were industry veterans like Dick Morgan and the Brown brothers based at remote Cygnet Bay experimenting with pearl cultivation, but with mixed results. One person getting close was Ian Turner from Broome Pearls, who was receiving tuition from a sympathetic Japanese technician called Mizno. Squire hoped that my visit might allow him to break the Japanese stranglehold on the business. Perhaps he hoped to play on historic resentments and alliances concerning the Japanese invasion of Burma in World War II.

I set off to Thailand from Perth, calling in first on my mate Dave Harris who by then was news director at Perth's Radio 6PR. He wrote me a reference which said that I was a stringer for the Major News Network, of which 6PR was then a member. He also asked me to file if I heard anything interesting.

Arriving in Bangkok, I decided the best place to pick up a news story was the Foreign Correspondents Club, which was then headquartered in swank Oriental Plaza. It was a Friday and the *Bangkok Post* had advertised an 'Australian Night'. I arrived at the club armed with my humble reference, but was rattled to see a tall, lanky, blond Australian inspecting members' ID at the door.

I offered my reference as evidence of my journalist credentials and he examined it thoroughly. 'Major News Network? Sorry mate, I've never heard of them. It's not Macquarie and it's not ABC. Who is this outfit?'

I stumbled and bumbled trying to justify my credentials but gave up, overcome by acute embarrassment and my awareness of the increasing exasperation of the queue of well heeled punters standing behind me. 'Look, I'm not really a journalist,' I finally admitted. 'I'm a Broome pearl diver on holidays and my mate gave me this reference in case I could file a radio story.'

'A pearl diver? Why didn't you tell me that in the first place? That's a damn sight more interesting than journalism. Follow me, and I'll shout you a book of beer tickets.'

And with that invitation, veteran combat cameraman Neil Davis grabbed my shoulder and ushered me to the bar.

My good fortune did not stop there. I was introduced to the Australian Trade Commissioner, Frank O'Brien, to whom I explained my ambitious mission to break the evil Japanese monopoly on cultured pearl techniques. He was amazed that any Australian wanted to do business in Rangoon. At this stage, Burma was still a relatively isolated nation, a one-party socialist state led by the repressive former general Ne Win. Nevertheless O'Brien treated my mission with interest and sympathy. He kindly offered the assistance of the Australian Embassy to arrange a meeting with the righteous sounding Burmese Peoples Pearl and Fisheries Corporation.

It got better. An American reporter from the AP wire service who had overheard our conversation thrust a business card into my hand with the request that I contact him when I returned from Rangoon. Pleased with this unexpected turn in my fortunes, I celebrated as any true pearl diver would – by getting totally smashed. My last memory was of heading off down Sukhumvit Road to a notorious haven of last resort, the Thermae Coffee Shop, along with Neil Davis, the ABC's resident correspondent, Paul Lockyer, and the BBC's Neil Kelly. There, if my vague recollection is correct, I recited selected verses from Banjo Paterson's 'Geebung Polo Club'.

Perhaps surprisingly, I got to Burma. In Rangoon I was picked up in an old, springless black embassy limo, and taken to meet an army major representing the country's Peoples Pearl and Fisheries Corporation. Despite my best efforts at diplomacy, he was predictably unenthusiastic about the prospect of losing pearl technicians to Australia. Even my appeals for a bilateral push against Japanese hegemony failed to move him. We both knew that any pearl operators he sent to Broome would probably have sought political asylum in order to escape the regime.

As I departed Rangoon's dilapidated airport, a very attractive Burmese immigration officer asked if I was from Perth. Knowing that the Western Australian capital has a big Anglo-Burmese émigré population, I replied in the affirmative. 'Oh I know Perth, that's where all the Burmese mongrels live,' she said. And with that she stamped my passport and flicked it back to me without a glance.

I had a few stories to tell back in the Roey, but none to file.

✻ ✻ ✻

Back in Broome I moved into new digs on a frangipani farm on the outskirts of town near Cable Beach. The property was owned by Sydney Mounsey, a former ABC-TV news editor, who had retired there with his doctor wife, an avowed communist who spent most of her time devoted to the urgent medical needs of remote Aboriginal communities. Syd could drive a tractor but that was about the extent of his skills around the farm. Big Bag knew him and introduced the two of us during a house call to fix a broken windmill pump.

Now that Ramah and I had split, I needed new accommodation. Syd offered to rent me a vacant caravan parked under a shady tree on the block. Back at the Barrow Pearls office I borrowed a welder and fabricated a steel tank stand from scraps lying round the yard. Shameless used an oxy torch to fix a tap into an old 200-litre drum which would serve as my bush shower. Syd was very impressed when I installed the water tower beside the caravan. My new home was now liveable.

It was an extraordinary piece of good fortune to have Syd as my landlord. He had been one of the senior journalists in the ABC's very first television newsroom back in Sydney in the fifties. As line-up sub-editor, he was in charge of news programming. So I had my first proper lessons in journalism from a master. Syd would give me a mess of scrambled copy with instructions to sort out the main facts and construct a news story. Once I had done my best, I left the typewritten copy under his door before heading back out to sea.

It was an unusual arrangement but a happy one, balancing my work as a pearl diver with my tutelage as a reporter.

THE LAST PEARLING LUGGER

On one memorable trip returning from the Lacepede Islands, Feeney drove the shallow draught lugger inshore on a high tide almost onto the beach. I leapt over the gunwales into the surf, my kitbag perched on my head, and waded back onto dry land. After a quick sprint across the hot sand dunes I was home. With prodding from Syd, who liked to remind me that I would be a mature-age entrant when I finally got a serious start in journalism, I began to plot my exit from pearl diving.

CHAPTER 16

Falling apart

When I put to sea again in early March 1983, I had already decided that this would be my last season on the luggers.

The *DMcD* was getting close to the end of her useful life. Years of heavy work had taken their toll on the venerable old lady. The electrics gave trouble constantly, the solenoid on the auto helm wouldn't work, the winch motor had seized, so it was back to hand-cranking the anchor first thing in the morning. Most importantly, the freezer would not freeze. Consequently, the mood among the crew was in contrast to the previous summer when we had happily worked out the season together. Now when shell patches became scarce, tensions rose and we all became gnarly.

An argument broke out about entitlement rights to the best diving position, generally considered to be the outside lines where a diver could swim out wide to gather more shell. I made the mistake of getting into a shoving match with Perry the paratrooper. A heavily muscled body builder and martial arts proponent, he was not nicknamed 'Charles Atlas' for nothing. I came off second best in our fisticuffs, which at least amused the drinkers in the Roebuck Bay's front bar when they learnt of it.

We put our differences aside, a reconciliation advanced when Perry was bitten by a stinger and, as ship's medic, I was summoned to administer first aid. But there was an issue. Both Big Bag and I were unconvinced that the big fella had been stung by an irukandji, so we withheld repeated requests for a shot of pethidine to put him out of his misery while we monitored his condition. Finally, Bruce got so tired of Perry's whining that he asked me to give him a shot to shut him up.

At the end of one neap, we received a radio request from Squire to proceed directly from the Eighty Mile Beach to Beagle Bay to try to find a lost dump of pearl shell. Floats marking the position had drifted off and it was our job to identify its location. Given that we were just returning after a fishing neap, food supplies were low and the idea of more diving as the tidal cycle changed was not popular. By the time we got to Beagle Bay the big spring tide would have arrived and the water would be well and truly disturbed, not a good time to be groping around the sea bottom.

The dump was in the entrance to the bay and the tide was already running in fast when Hard Porn Holmes and

THE LAST PEARLING LUGGER

I were asked to do the first drift. It was one of the spookiest dives ever. Visibility was less than a metre and, though we were working in only about fifteen metres of water, it was late in the day – feeding time for a whole swag of carnivores bigger, hungrier and much less well mannered than us. In addition to the eternal hazard of tiger sharks, several saltwater crocodiles had recently been sighted by the local Aboriginal community who fished and lived around the bay.

In the gloom, I gripped my work line tightly, hugging as close as I could to the shot weight which I could not see, but which I could sense crashing into lumps of coral ahead of me – all very unnerving. Through a cloud of silty water I passed over several sawfish, big bottom-dwelling invertebrates related to sharks, with a flattened snout with jagged edges just like a chainsaw. They scootered off into the murkiness as I floated over them. I also thought I saw flashes of silver-coloured underbelly, always an alarming sign of bigger sharks around.

I was being towed fast and low over coral bottom trying to spot the pearl shell dump when suddenly I found myself looking at a huge set of eyes staring back at me only inches away – a giant ray. I don't know which of us took off first, but there was a massive explosion of sand underneath me as the monster began to crank up his powerful triangular wing. My heart felt like it was vibrating out of its rib cage by this stage, and that was the final straw. I went straight to the top. It was hardly surprising to see Hard Porn already on deck stripped out of his wetsuit and furiously chain smoking. He was spooked worse than me.

We both agreed that there was no way we were going back in the water – a message colourfully and unambiguously conveyed to Big Bag. It worked. The search was abandoned. Big Bag radioed Steve to say the dump was lost and we set course south back to Broome. The return trip was memorable. We had run out of cooking gas and aside from some fish we had caught in Beagle Bay we were out of tucker. But we could improvise. We had some firewood and an old oil drum. We hacked the top of the drum and chopped some vents in the bottom before sitting it on three bricks over a sheet of tin behind the helm on the stern of the lugger. We stuffed the drum with toilet tissue and the firewood but discovered we had run out of matches. Feeney found a can of aero-start in the engine room. Giving our fire box a good spray of the explosive fuel we lugged up a battery and produced a spark which ignited our fire with a thumping flash.

Soon we had a huge blaze which must have presented a strange sight to the clusters of scattered campers we passed at Quandong and Barred Creek. It was night and all they would have seen was the navigation lights of the *DMcD* and a huge fire with flames and smoke streaming off the lugger's stern. If anything it would have just added to the legend of the *DMcD*. At least we were able to brew up a billy and heat some food.

Back in Broome, we beached on the foreshore in front of the Roey prior to anti-fouling the hull. It was an opportunity to rectify some of the boat's more critical problems before we returned to the Eighty Mile pearling grounds and the deep water.

* * *

THE LAST PEARLING LUGGER

APART FROM Farley and the crew of the *Roebuck Pearl*, we were the only boat working out deep at the start of the '83 season. Deep water tested our primal fears. There was fear of the bends, of a burst hose or snap connector on the regulator blowing off, fear of drowning, or of sudden blackouts, and of course fear of the critter factor. We all had our own pet anxieties. Shameless Shane used to fret about spewing under water from nausea or indigestion from a crook breakfast. With good reason, given my memories of the *Pacific Lady*, I used to spook myself about experiencing a kinked hose on the last dive of the day in 20 fathoms. No diver relished making an emergency ascent in a nitrogen-saturated body. Such was the fear that several of us began practising free ascents between drifts, in order to build up our stamina.

By the time the *DMcD* joined Farley's *Roebuck Pearl* down over the Compass Rose site, his crew had worked more than a full season in the deep water. Ever the pioneer, he had finetuned his dive tables using oxygen to fast-track the absorption of residual nitrogen in the bloodstream. We copied Farley's dive tables or close enough, Big Bag adjusting them as he saw fit. It was perilous diving – at least 40 metres even on low tide.

The *DMcD* used two teams of three divers, which allowed one team to recuperate on deck while the other one was down. Dives were timed for 25 minutes bottom time, six per day. We ended with a two-hour hang-off on the last dive of the day, supplemented by oxygen once we passed the 17-metre mark. Oxygen is an aid to diver recuperation if taken at depths less than 17 metres; at greater depths it is toxic.

I quickly noticed the effect of deep-diving on my physical condition. I would emerge from a deep dive feeling giddy and buzzing internally as though wired into a low voltage battery pack. But Big Bag was so impressed with the success of 'his' dive table that he urged me in my capacity as resident journalist to write to the Royal Australian Navy's head of medicine advising of our remarkable scientific breakthrough in extending bottom time in 35-metre dives by more than several hours per day.

Two months later we got a reply, which Big Bag promptly stabbed to the mast with his diving knife, a sure indication it was not the answer that he had expected. We gathered round to read the offending minute. 'Dear Mr Barker, Thank you for your recent suggestion proposing changes to Navy's Admiralty Dive Tables – I'm amazed I haven't met you in the Coroners Court.' It was signed by the navy's chief medico. Big Bag told me later that the letter had been filed in the company's records in Broome, but I somehow doubt it.

By the middle of the season, the PPL fleet luggers had finished fishing live shell in the traditional 'potato patch' off Mangrove Point, and came out to join us on the Compass Rose. Badger, at least in the beginning, opted for long hang-offs without oxygen, without rotating his divers. His crew were hit hard from the bends and blamed it on Badger's dive tables.

Wonder Dog was constantly getting bent. Unable to sleep at night from pain, he was forced to go back into the water for a prolonged hang-off. 'Mick Bray and I especially suffered the bends. I was getting bent at one in the morning, usually in my knee. I'd have to wake Badge up.

THE LAST PEARLING LUGGER

He'd drop a shot weight over the side and that was it – I would have to struggle back into my wet suit and go over the side to hang-off.'

Some nights it was dead calm but when the westerlies were blowing it was a nightmare. 'With the lugger rolling, the shot weight tied off the outrigger would be flying up and down and you had to be extremely careful it didn't hit you. Once it just narrowly missed taking my head off.' Badger's habit of shining a light into the water to check on the diver's condition during nocturnal decompression was not welcomed. 'We knew the mother of all tiger sharks lived out there and if a big shark came through I did not want to see it.'

Some divers were so loaded with nitrogen that just the simple act of descending the forward companionway to climb into their bunks would often result in a jarred knee and bring on a bender. The first resort was usually a painkiller but if the ache inevitably worsened there was no option but to suit up and go over side. We called them Panadol parties.

In bad cases, hanging off meant staying in the water for as long as four or five hours, staging a slow ascent and finally clambering out as the sun rose, marking the start of another diving day. It was around this time the expression 'salt water cowboys' started making the rounds of the pearling fleet – a reference to our seemingly mad risk taking.

Even our deep competition among divers for the highest shell catch was intense. Divers became fierce adversaries, fighting over every pearl shell that lay between them, scrambles which became particularly adversarial if shell counts were low. Masks would often get ripped off in underwater tussles. The damage done to shell stocks by years of overfishing was beginning to show. While we could often make good money in the deep water, the pickings were not consistent and our pay packets at the end of each neap's fishing varied considerably. Even working deep water, the pearl shell patches were scattered and returns were barely enough to cover costs. As the 1983 season progressed our tallies began to decline.

Frustrations began to spill over. Cartoons critical of the allocation of resources for the boat, as opposed to the funds spent on setting up the new Beagle Bay pearl farm, started appearing in the lugger's shell book, a register of the individual tallies for the neap. The *DMcD* needed a major refit but money was tight and personal relations between Steve and Big Bag were increasingly ragged. A split was looming. Feeney and Shameless were talking about moving on, Feeney down south back to crayfishing and Shane to Darwin and a job driving mackerel dories in the Timor Sea.

It was the death of nineteen-year-old John Battersby, the karate kid from Newcastle, that cemented my own plans to check out of pearling; particularly the haste with which the circumstances surrounding his disappearance were so hastily and conveniently swept away – almost as if he never existed.

It was the last day of a neap and the *Roebuck Pearl* was drift fishing in ten fathoms, having moved north after scant pickings around the Turtle Islands at the southern end of the Eighty Mile. Weather was dead calm and head diver Salty Dog and co-divers Steve Oats and John

Battersby were on deck. John wanted to practise his free diving and donned his fins, weight belt and mask before descending the divers' ladder. After several minutes had elapsed Salty noticed that the Bat had not surfaced from several practice dives. He and Oats conferred and decided that John was probably on the bottom 'buddy breathing' (sharing a regulator) with Mark Walsh. More minutes passed, and the crew on deck tugged the divers' lines, signalling it was time to stop fishing and come to the surface. Up came the shell bags, bobbing on the water, followed by the scheduled divers. But there was no sign of John Battersby.

Salty, by now very worried, asked Walshy, the last diver up, if he had sighted the Bat below. He had, but not for at least six minutes. Worry turned to panic. A marker flag was dropped; meanwhile, the crew searched the boat for any sign that he had come back on board unnoticed. 'We got on top of the wheelhouse with binoculars. It was dead, dead calm and we were expecting to see him waving at us but it was just a clear empty sea,' Salty told me later.

At that point, Salty says he first suggested to Farley to radio the *Pacific Lady* and the *Paspaley I* which were nearby, and to request help for a search. According to Salty, Farley disagreed, saying it was better not to get the other boats involved.

The *Roebuck Pearl* was again readied for diving, and for the rest of the day its crew mounted a fruitless search for the Bat, although by now they knew that if he was still underwater then they were looking for a corpse. By the end of the day the water was very cloudy. It was the end of the neap tide cycle.

With darkness falling, the diving gear was packed and the boat prepared for a return to Broome. On the way home there was a bizarre celebration because it was Farley's birthday. Salty Dog still has a photo of that evening. After dropping anchor in Broome around noon the following day, Farley drove down to the Broome police station to notify them the boat had come home a diver short. No further search was ever launched and if any action was taken against Farley, I was unaware of it and so were most of the other divers. We felt it was as if the Bat had never existed.

Six weeks later some people from the community at Lagrange Bay found a diving bootie complete with ankle bone, washed up along the Eighty Mile Beach. Scraps of diving attire and bits of wetsuit were also found in the area. They included the remnants of a pair of socks bearing the logo of a Newcastle football club, which the Bat had been wearing to pad out his flippers when he went missing.

We knew that it was unlikely that he had been taken by a shark, because no one had sighted one in the water at the time. Though the teeth marks on the wet suit indicated his corpse had been mauled, that probably came later, and the most likely explanation for his death was that he blacked out from the exertion of free diving, perhaps moments after waving at Mark Walsh underwater.

The subsequent inquest found death by accident. 'I don't believe we would have ever found John alive but I do believe if we'd called in those other companies, the chances of bringing home a body would have increased dramatically,' Salty told me sadly.

THE LAST PEARLING LUGGER

John's mate Larry House organised with the Shire for a memorial to be erected at Town Beach, the embarkation point for our fishing trips.

It reads: 'John Battersby, Lost at sea, 21 September, 1983: Gone but not forgotten.'

* * *

WHEN I looked back over my record on the pearling luggers, even I could see that I was a proverbial boat hopper. I had resigned or been sacked so many times that from 1979 until 1983 I held the record for the number of pearling boats worked by a deckhand/diver, a feat of dubious seamanship that probably still stands today. Nevertheless, I had always bobbed up again, able to find employment on another boat.

Before I checked out of Broome, I did one last trip on the newly commissioned *Paspaley II*, the last word in Japanese fibreglass ship design. Genial Tofe Cleveland was the skipper, a former RAN officer who was commander of an Attack Class patrol boat based at Darwin when Cyclone Tracy hit. He and his crew managed to keep her afloat through the catastrophic monsoon, a rare achievement. All the others bar one sank after being caught at sea.

Tofe had brought along his old patrol boat engineer Harry, although the *Paspaley II* was a far cry from a gun boat. It was a luxurious life and easy going, involving some fishing and dump collecting.

It was on one of the last days out that I caught a big stonefish lying on the bottom. A truly ugly brute, and one of the largest I had ever seen, the fish was lying in open garden bottom and was easy prey. I scooped him up with my neck bag, deciding then and there to name him Dad, after my favourite lugger skipper.

I intended to donate him to Salty Dog's Aquarium of Aquatic Horror. But unfortunately Dad died a premature and ignominious death of exposure, after he was left sweltering on deck in a plastic prawn bin. Tofe, appreciating the gravity of my loss, ordered all hands on deck for a Burial at Sea and a funeral oration, then the stonefish's rapidly deteriorating remains were consigned to the deep.

CHAPTER 17

The end of an era

By late 1983, Broome was starting to change rapidly. In the last few months before I left for good, it was clear that the developers were moving in. Lord Alistair McAlpine, an English peer with an eclectic range of business interests, had purchased a residence in Broome and was starting to develop his tourism and property interests there. Soon even the Bond Corporation would start snapping up historic blocks. All this was altering the character of the community, as locals who worked in the pearling industry were pushed further out by rising property prices.

It was hard to believe that Broome had been a real frontier town only twenty years before. There were few bitumen roads and the place lacked sewerage or drainage, relied on tank water and kerosene refrigeration, and was largely dependent for fruit, vegetables and groceries on the ship that came in every fortnight. Don McKenzie remembered catching kangaroos in the bush around Chinatown to help feed his family.

In the seventies, with the sealing of the region's highways, many improvements to everyday life became possible. Better roads also brought more tourists – 'terrorists' as some locals dubbed them – and by the early eighties, the tourist boom was upon the town. At least McAlpine was interested in preserving the town's authentic heritage. He was very critical of the decision to demolish Bishop's Palace, and set out to do what he could to prevent such vandalism happening again. His efforts ensured the preservation of the McDaniel residence, among other historic buildings. It was a different attitude from the traditional white bosses of Broome. You would see them in the private bar of the Conti, the pearling masters, the local councillors and the professional men, hatching their plans for 'progress'.

The last house I lived in before I left was one marked for redevelopment. It was a corrugated iron cottage – a shed, really – shared with Perry the paratrooper, his girlfriend and Gus, Big Bag's younger brother who worked for the shire. The accommodation was temporary, but comfortable enough and cheap. I bought a bail of hessian cloth which I stapled to the interior as a cheap wall lining, then I found some pallets which made a comfortable bed base. A fan and desk completed the furnishings.

When we had to go, we held a big party to mark our eviction, purchasing four kegs of beer which we hooked up together and christened 'Dense Pack' in homage

THE LAST PEARLING LUGGER

to US President Ronald Reagan's anti-nuclear deterrent strategy. A visiting blues band from Perth provided the entertainment, and to feed the troops we dug a massive hangi and filled it with old lumps of anchor chain instead of rocks. The food cages held whole chickens, whole steamed fish, turtle (we had many indigenous guests) and beef cuts. The shindig lasted for days, and was one of the last occasions on which the pearling crews as I knew them were all together.

Shameless Shane was already gone. A few months before, he had dropped by my caravan at Syd's place. I was fast asleep and was woken by loud banging on the caravan door. Shane was standing there, covered in windscreen glass and dozens of tiny cuts. He had come with a dozen stubbies so we sat down for a drink and he explained what had happened.

A furious argument had erupted between Shane and his latest girlfriend, Audrey, after a prolonged session at the Roebuck which had ended with Shane trying to auction her off. She stormed off across the road to the Sandfly apartments, followed shortly thereafter by Shane, who decided to grab the keys to the car and go for a drive. As he backed down the driveway, Audrey sprang out from behind some bushes where she had been waiting, and heaved a spare tyre through the windscreen of the vehicle. She was a formidable woman; but then, Shameless was a formidable man.

He had the clothes he was in and that was about all; nevertheless, he had decided to leave Broome. Departure that night was out of the question, so he crashed on a couch outside the van. The next morning I accompanied him into town to find a temporary windscreen for the long drive ahead. There was nothing at Burglar Bill's, the service station of last resort at the edge of town, so he bought an outrageous pair of sunglasses instead, and after fuelling up he exited Broome with a screeching driveway burnout. A week later I heard that he had made it to Darwin in one piece.

Big Bag had also decided that it was time to leave. He checked out of town in his old green ute, returning to Onslow to embark on a new pearling venture there with Lindsay Brady, a former police officer. His departure was sudden, and without any farewells, in many ways in keeping with his character. No fuss, just a need to put the past behind him quickly and get on with life.

Other pearling workers were leaving town because PPL's future had started to look shaky. Rumours that PPL was in financial trouble were nothing new. We were all aware of the toll wrought by pearl shell disease at their remote Kimberley coast farm at Kuri Bay. We knew from crew on board the company mother ships, *Kuri Pearl* and *Merinda Pearl*, which ferried the live shell from the grounds to the farm that the hygiene of the ships' rusty holding tanks was probably to blame. Farley had for ages warned about the lack of cleanliness on board the veteran ships, but many people in the industry obviously did not understand the issue as well as he did.

What no one outside the company had been aware of was the extent to which the disease and spiralling costs were hurting PPL's bottom line. One dramatic day midway through the '83 pearling season, the managing director of PPL, Alec Myer, came up from Perth and gathered the company's Broome employees together. He told the assembled divers and slipway workers that the company was bankrupt and save for a handful of staff they were to be laid off. The skippers, who were independent contractors, would not have their contracts renewed.

My old mate Wonder Dog, a PPL diver, was there to hear the news. 'The shut down was pretty much temporary, but came across as worse than it really was,' he told me later. In time, most of the divers and maintenance gangs would be back at work. In the meantime, some employees – particularly the indigenous workers in the boatshed – lost the only job that they had ever known.

The bad news spread like lightning through Broome. Another of my mates, Greg Nichol, had just got into town that morning after driving all night from Geraldton to take up a diving job offer with Dad – only to be told there was now no job. He took the only sensible course of action – headed to the Roey and got pissed. As for Dad himself, well, the blow fell hard on the PPL skippers, who were lugger owners and independent contractors. I remember seeing Dad's car parked in the driveway of Barrow Pearls, as he rushed around to see Squire and Big Bag, inquiring whether they needed help fishing their quota (they didn't).

As for me, when the lads emerged from the meeting and spilled out the details, I had my first news story and quite a scoop at that: Western Australia's oldest and best known pearling company was broke! After confirming the details with Myer, who offered a short tersely worded statement, I rushed home to retrieve my portable typewriter, and belted out a story. Then I rang it through to a grateful sub-editor on the *West Australian*, who was surprised, if pleased, to find out that the paper had a 'stringer' in Broome with such a detailed knowledge of the pearling industry.

Eventually, the independent skippers were able to regroup, and supply PPL with smaller quotas, but the company had been rocked to its foundations, and uncertainty marked the days ahead. Along the way the luggers themselves became redundant, as operators like Badger took up using small steel trawlers. Gradually, the luggers were sold off. The last luggers to operate out of Broome were the ones skippered by the Japanese, and by the end of the eighties their era was over too.

* * *

When it came my turn to leave Broome, like Big Bag I did not have much to pack. Apart from my diving gear, the sum of my possessions was a few clothes, my precious Nikkormat camera, some boxes of slides documenting my five years in the old pearling port – and the rudder of a schooner. I had found the rudder when I was working on the B-6, and it was docked alongside Streeters Jetty. A massive spring tide had lifted the old rudder from the clutches of the mangroves where it had lain undisturbed for decades.

This large, cumbersome object was the first item that I tried to load into the back of the Land Cruiser, a potent symbol of my next voyage into the unknown. The build up to the wet season had begun, and I was soon soaked in perspiration from the exertion. I dragged the rudder to the end of the jetty and tied it off, thinking I would return later and collect it. It was huge, too big to have come off

THE LAST PEARLING LUGGER

a lugger, and had probably once been part of the steering gear of a schooner or mother ship.

Then I tossed the rest of my clobber into the back, roped it down, and headed off to the Roebuck Bay Hotel where I had arranged to meet Ronnie Ugle, Walshy's former girlfriend, who wanted a lift down to Perth. At the Roey, friends came and went, shouting jugs of beer and bottles of champagne which we sprayed all over the place. What had been planned as a quick pit stop turned into a raging boozy farewell party.

The sun was setting when Ronnie and I finally drove off down Dampier Terrace passing the familiar landmarks of Chinatown: the shuttered office of Pearls Pty Ltd, Streeters' hardware, the quaint little shop belonging to L.L. Tacks, Tang Wei's famous long soup restaurant still lit in garish green neon as it had been when Al and I were first beckoned inside five years earlier. Turning right out of town I passed the old DC-3 which served as the local tourist office for the increasing hordes of visitors. Crossing the pindan flats I was escorted for a few moments by a flock of fruit bats wheeling over the mangroves on their nightly hunt for food.

Ronnie soon nodded off, but I was too energised, my brain in overload as I contemplated a new life ahead. There was no certain future and I was dogged by the nagging uncertainty of my venture. I had only a little spare cash – 1983 had been a fiscal fiasco. The only thing I had in any real quantity was hope.

At the Sandfire Roadhouse about 300 kilometres south of Broome, we stopped to refuel. I put on a cassette and wound the window down to try and freshen up, but I was very tired and found it hard to concentrate on the long straight road ahead. Eventually, I passed a sign pointing to Eighty Mile Beach. It must have been close to the Three Sandhills, that definitive landmark which I had last seen from the deck of the *DMcD* – a most auspicious camp spot, I thought. I turned the Land Cruiser off on a sandy track which wound in for several kilometres until the headlights caught the base of a high ridge of sand dunes. Then I turned off the engine and listened to the soothing crash of surf in the distance.

It was a warm night, so we would sleep under the stars. First, a quick check for snakes before I spread out the ground sheet, an old foam mattress and a blanket. As if in a sleep walk, Ronnie stumbled out of the cab and fell onto the mattress – out like a light. I scrambled up the face of the dune to the summit, where there was a cooling sea breeze.

I don't know how long I sat on the dune staring out to sea, my head swirling in memories of years spent out there. I remembered all the good times I had had on the *DMcD*, not just the company, but my initiation into the experience of life at sea on a lugger. How, on one of my last trips on the *DMcD*, I had seen a whale while I was on watch one night when we were sailing back to port.

I was taking a radar fix to make sure we were still on course when I noticed a 'blip' on the screen. It was after midnight and the rest of the crew were down below, dozing or asleep. I double-checked the ship's position and went back to the chart to ensure there were no reefs or obstacles marked. The course was good and as I came up on the mystery target I grabbed the binoculars for a better look: under the moonlight, on a dead calm sea, an adult humpback was standing on its head, only its massive fluked tail protruding as it gorged on krill floating in the tide. I switched off the autopilot, throttled back the engine and quietly pointed the lugger in the direction of the whale, the rest of the crew eventually joining me on deck. The lugger nosed within 50 metres of the leviathan, then it flopped over on its side, disappearing into the inky ocean depths.

* * *

IN SILENT contemplation, I reflected how little this coastline had changed since the luggermen had arrived in the nineteenth century. I thought of the thousands of crew who had perished at sea, whose broken bodies had washed up here on this very shore.

A waning crescent moon hung high in the starry heavens, and the only noise was the resounding, relentless ocean.

EPILOGUE:

Turning for port

Broome, 2003. Twenty years after my last drift I was back, joining a mixed bunch of locals who gathered at sundown one humid October evening to farewell one of the town's most colourful seafarers. Mannie Manolas had died at the age of seventy-three and another link with Broome's history was gone.

His pearling days had been well behind him by the time I got to know the old sea dog. In 1983, the last place I lived in before I checked out of Broome was a three-bedroom tin shed in Walcott Street, close to Mannie's old style Broome bungalow just down the road.

In truth, Mannie had been much closer to Big Bag and Squire than he was to me. They were the keepers of many of his secrets – the tricks of lugger maintenance, a lifetime's intelligence about the best pearl shell grounds, and the danger spots to avoid. Still, when I got the news that he was dying, something impelled me to make a 2000-kilometre dash down from Darwin, where I was working for the ABC. I'd had the successful career in journalism that I'd wanted, been to many interesting places, and served as a correspondent in some hot corners of Southeast Asia. Yet, I'd never really been able to let go of my links to Broome and its pearling industry which had given me five of the most memorable years of my life.

Pretty much all I knew about the last few years of Mannie's existence was that they had not been easy. In 1998, at the age of sixty-eight, he was busted by the police for trafficking marijuana. Any defence that he was just a dotty old pensioner was blown after a loaded .357 Magnum was found under his pillow. Jailed for fifteen months, he was deemed too ill for prison and allowed home detention. Well, living in Broome, he wasn't going to escape anywhere.

The sun had well and truly set by the time my old Land Cruiser arrived in town. Even in the darkness it was clear how much Broome had changed since my last visit. I was startled to see a garish McDonald's sign and a set of golden arches where Burglar Bill's service station had once stood at the entrance to town. I camped the night on the rural block that Big Bag owned at Yamashita Drive, then called around to Mannie's house next day.

He was a hard nut to the end, I concluded, as I read the hand-scrawled note taped to his bedroom door requesting that nobody pray for him except Father Pelle.

THE LAST PEARLING LUGGER

The old bloke was propped up on pillows, dozing. I struggled to recognise the emaciated body in front of me. He'd always been a man of action, as the old photos and drawings pinned on the walls attested: Mannie as fisherman, horse trainer, engineer, roustabout. Now he was dying of advanced emphysema and associated infection, and a palliative-care nurse administered him a daily shot of morphine.

He was drifting in and out of consciousness, so I stayed for fifteen minutes or so, chatting to him about the days when I was a pearl diver on the luggers. I reminded him of the first time I'd ever sighted him, a stiff sou'easter blowing as his barra boat, the *Dawn*, escorted a little convoy of Vietnamese refugee boats into the safety of Roebuck Bay, like a mother duck anxiously herding her chicks.

When I got up to leave, 'Don't go' he whispered, his thin hand gripping my wrist. So I sat down again, and recalled how Mannie swore it was ASIO spies who had sunk the *Dawn* in Roebuck Bay in 1982, payback for help he had given East Timorese after Indonesia invaded the former Portuguese colony seven years before. At the time, many of the drinkers in the front bar of the Roey had pooh-poohed these claims. But in 1999 I was based in East Timor as a journalist covering the historic independence vote and met a former Falintil guerilla commander who claimed to have known Mannie and identified him by his surname, Manolas, so my mind remains open. And just the year before Mannie died, the Labor MP Warren Snowdon made a speech in federal parliament about Australia's attitude to the invasion of East Timor, in which he praised Mannie's involvement:

There was also a core of activists from the non-Timorese community in the Top End, some of whom took great personal risk – people such as Mannie Manolas who, with three others, sailed his boat, *The Dawn*, out of Darwin bound for East Timor. With Mannie on the boat were Rob Wesley-Smith, Jim Zantis and Cliff Morrow.

The purpose of their voyage was to deliver medical and other supplies. The boat was seized by Customs and they were arrested while they were still in Australian waters. They were held in jail overnight and then were put before a court. Their defence lawyer was successful in getting weapons smuggling charges withdrawn. They were bailed and eventually found guilty and released on bonds.

Mannie Manolas was charged with leaving port without clearance and his boat was confiscated and badly damaged. He applied to Customs for it to be returned. He was offered $7000 compensation, although it had cost $30,000 to fix. He was eventually made a 'take it or leave it' offer of $14,000.

So perhaps there was some sort of truth in Mannie's claims.

He was certainly fondly regarded by the East Timorese community in Darwin, who presented his family with a beautiful hand-woven traditional Tais cloth as a funeral gift.

Anyway, back to the *Dawn*. In late '82 in the middle of the Wet, my old crew mates Big Bag, Squire and Feeney raised the *Dawn*. After locating the wreck off Town Beach, they scrounged fifty-four empty fuel drums which they sank around the hulk, which was resting on its side in 50 feet of water on the bottom of Roebuck Bay.

Using compressor-driven airlines, they tied the drums to the boat, then used regulators to blow the water out of them. As much to their surprise as anyone's else, the old scow, all 20 metres of her, rose slowly off the bottom. She was towed up Dampier Creek and beached on the foreshore outside the Sandfly Apartments.

There she lay for several months. At one point Feeney and I even considered buying her to fish barramundi. But on closer inspection we decided that she needed too much work to be made seaworthy, so we let the mangroves claim her. Months later Squire got jack of the hulk, which had become a home for local itinerants. He burnt it. I was slightly shocked when I read later in a state maritime list that the *Dawn*'s keel had been laid as far back as 1920. Another piece of Broome history obliterated.

❋ ❋ ❋

DESPITE HIS misgivings about religion, Mannie was given a Christian burial. A well attended service was held at St Mary's, followed by a memorable wake at the Pearl Luggers exhibition, a permanent display set in a beautiful tropical garden redolent with the heavy perfume of frangipani. The star exhibits were the last of the luggers, the *Kim* and the legendary *DMcD*, now dry docked in the garden. On this night, the *DMcD*'s sails were hoisted, and a group of local musicians gathered on deck playing ballads to Mannie's memory. I remembered how Mannie's son Mick, a guitarist, had hung out with us at the Palace, those Sunday afternoon jam sessions on the back verandah.

There were many familiar faces: Kim Male, 'the man in white', a childhood friend of Mannie's who remembered him as the terror of the northwest town. Old Hamaguchi and his wife Pearl, and the other veteran divers, Paulie Phillips and Eddy Roe, all survivors of the bends and some still carrying the scars. Dave Dureau, son of Keith Dureau, almost a Robinson Crusoe figure in tattered shorts, summer shirt and a disconcertingly pair of bright red socks.

And my own mob, if not too many of them. Squire, Zimmo, Salty Dog and Kenny Buckeridge, son of the lugger builder whose slipway and shack once stood on this very site. As the evening progressed I began to recognise even more faces that I hadn't seen for more than twenty years. I turned at a gentle tap on the shoulder. It was my old friend and housemate, Mindau.

Together, over a few more beers, we all pondered the effect of pearls on the human condition.

Much had changed in the Broome pearling industry since I left in 1983. PPL's star had terminally declined, and Paspaley's had risen. These changes began at Otto Gerdau, the old commodities firm in New York which had been a founding partner in PPL. The American company had held a stake in Broome's pearling industry since the early twentieth century. During the first phase of the Great Depression, it effectively bailed out the industry, purchasing the bulk of the catch. After the war, when pearling was starting up again, it once again played a prominent role in Broome's fortunes, in 1949 contracting with leading pearlers to buy almost the entire production of pearl shell in that year and the two years following.

Over time, there was considerable grumbling from Australians about the New York firm's near monopoly. Pearlers resented the way prices were controlled, while those who opposed Japanese investment in Australia after World War II resented Gerdau's other investments in Japanese pearling ventures. One Australian journalist who had covered the Australian Army's desperate Kokoda campaign sarcastically dubbed the firm's principal, Allan Gerdau, 'the man who buttons up the shirt of America'. The economic health and social development of Broome was inextricably bound up with this powerful company on the other side of the world.

The firm of Otto Gerdau eventually acquired Brown and Dureau's 24 per cent stake in PPL, giving it a 52 per cent majority holding in the Australian entity. But when Allan Gerdau died in 1986 at the age of eighty-seven, for reasons best known only to himself he deeded his entire estate to church interests – one third each to the Episcopalian Church, the Catholic Church and a Jewish synagogue. This ownership change was further complicated by a rotating management agreement among the three churches each taking their turn to oversee the running of the group.

Not surprisingly in the circumstances, in 1988 there was a move by a son-in-law to take the firm of Otto Gerdau back from the churches. This move was supported by PPL. In January 1989 Kim Male and PPL's operations manager, Neville Crane, went to New York with a bold plan to convince the church group, at the time led by the synagogue, to sell their holdings. But their bid was regarded as too low and was rejected.

PPL's failed management buyout did not go unnoticed at the Paspaley Pearling Company's headquarters in Darwin. Paspaley was by now about five times as productive as PPL and ten times more profitable. Nick Paspaley junior had a friend obtain a copy of the Gerdau will and then contacted its beneficiaries for a meeting. With help from a Jewish business friend, George Levin, who had rendered assistance during the building of *Paspaley IV* at the Nishii Shipyard in Japan, Nick discovered the church coalition was dissatisfied with PPL's buyout offer. 'I offered to make an offer under the condition that they would agree to sit in a locked room until a deal was agreed, or until we both walked away from the deal,' he told me later. 'By the end of the day we had a signed heads of agreement giving me three months to close the deal. Consequently the PPL management buyout offer was dismissed on the signing of my agreement.'

When the spoils were eventually shared, for his efforts Levin ended up with 4000 acres of pristine North Carolina farmland complete with 'gentleman's retreat'. Nick Paspaley found himself in control of a prime fourteen-storey office building in New York's Wall Street precinct, running from Pearl Street to Water Street. The Gerdau estate also included an old master pearler's residence in Broome, PPL's packing sheds, Japanese divers' quarters and adjacent single men's residence, and the lugger maintenance yards and slipway. Add to that the historic Streeters Jetty, the small historic wooden pier. Most of these old working structures were later demolished, leaving a gaping space in Broome's pearling history.

THE LAST PEARLING LUGGER

In the ensuing years Paspaley went from strength to strength, buying up small and large pearl companies, including Farley's interests. It had ended up controlling about 80 per cent of the industry. In 1990, Kim Male sold his remaining interests to Paspaley and began a new, more modest cultured pearl venture in the Northern Territory, selling out in 2005 to Arafura Pearls. He also retained control of the historic general trading company, Streeter and Male, which maintained a commercial presence in Broome.

What of the other people I had known in pearling? Quite a few ended up wealthy, including Farley. These days he lives in Europe and skis at Aspen, Colorado. Then there was John Kelly, who had kept quiet about his asthma condition, got past his diving medicals and taken over my old diving job on the B-6. He went on to earn a seven-figure sum as chief executive of the Paspaley group. Once he made his money, he promptly retired, to spend his time sailing the South Seas for pleasure.

Things had also worked out well for my close friends Norm and Karen, who had settled near Castlemaine in central Victoria and raised a family. Karen resumed nursing while Norm studied information technology, eventually landing a job as onboard systems operator for a company that conducted aerial seismic surveys. Hard to believe, but it was a job with an even higher wipeout factor than pearl diving. His work has taken him around Australia, to Africa and the Middle East. Shameless eventually moved to Fremantle, upgraded his skippers ticket and got work driving thousand-tonne barges carrying oil drilling equipment for the northwest shelf.

Ever the larrikin, he built a mini fishing trawler for his kids, complete with echo sounder, radar and radio liberated from a previous employer.

But more than one of my friends had struggled. Bazza Thorpe's end was tragic. Life after his necrosis diagnosis was difficult. He and Carol moved to Perth where one morning while he was swimming at Cottesloe Beach he was struck by a wayward surfboard and suffered a major head wound. An increasingly angry and bitter young man, he split with Carol, who moved back to Melbourne while he stayed in the West. During celebrations at the America's Cup defence at Fremantle in 1987, he apparently partied too hard, suffered a major seizure and was found dead in bed, face down.

Now Salty Dog, talented head diver, was also struggling with the ravages of necrosis. He had thrown in the diving, and was working in Broome, running a tour bus and doing other jobs.

Some of my other friends had turned to drugs and alcohol, including a close mate who went into selling heroin futures, was caught and copped a couple of years of porridge to straighten him out. One found religion, and gave away most of his assets to the church, before deciding he had made a serious error.

At least I didn't have to worry about Big Bag. I'd caught up with him on my way over to Broome. Despite building a comfortable bank balance from his time in pearling, my old skipper had not opted for a relaxed retirement. He was developing an eco resort at his farm at Parry's Creek outside Wyndham, and also had a mango farm to tend to in Broome. If any one was going to be all right, I figured, it was Big Bag.

How wrong I was. Just a couple of years after Mannie's death, Bruce hanged himself on the porch at his Wyndham farm, a jump off the verandah, about the same height as the old diving ladder on the *DMcD*. One thing for sure, the hangman's knot was never going to come undone. He'd made sure of that.

* * *

MEN WHO have lived full lives ending their own lives: it's not such an uncommon story in the wild northwest. Not too long after Bruce checked out, one of his best friends, Graham Hutton, a talented geologist and bushman, and a director of Kimberley Diamonds, drove to the race track with a six-pack and a gun, drank the beer, and then shot himself in the heart.

Depression was the official reason given for Big Bag's death. I preferred to remember Bruce as I had last seen him, a couple of days before Mannie's funeral. He seemed the same as ever, dressed in shearer's singlet and shorts, just as he would have been for a day of anti-fouling the lugger in the mangroves of Dampier Creek two decades earlier. He was over sixty by then, and unimpressed that his knees were getting stiffer and that his eyes troubled him. Otherwise, he struck me as pretty content. He had worked hard to turn his farm at Parry's Creek into an eco resort, with impressive results: there was a skywalk around the lagoons, and cabins. The place was on the tourist map.

Of all my mates from the luggers, Bruce was one I'd particularly stayed in touch with. In our lugger days, he shied away from town. He'd rather be on his block, or back on the boat working. Seeing his labour bear fruit was one of his great pleasures. Yet he was not one of those reclusive bushies – far from it. Over the years I spent a fair bit of time with him, helping at his Onslow pearl farm, or on the mango farm at Broome. He loved a good yabber – about the women we'd both known, my work overseas as a correspondent, and what had become of old friends like Steve and Mark Feeney.

Like an older brother, he'd bailed me out of the Fremantle police lock-up when I once got into a fight, and when I was awarded a five-acre block near Derby, he came had helped me fence it. Being Bruce, he showed me how to do it from scratch: chopping down trees and splitting their timber to make fencing posts.

This personal resourcefulness was one of the qualities that I admired most in Big Bag. Another was his quiet determination to see the job through. Once, when I was down on his pearl farm at Onslow, he decided he wanted to check a pearl dump. It was right out near the Mackerel Islands. We went out in the farm boat, an old assault boat that was really just a very heavy dinghy with big engines. The weather gradually turned rough and it was becoming dark, so we put ashore on the island. We had supplies with us, boiled a billy on the beach, and made camp for the night. At midnight, as the weather deteriorated and the storm got up, without a word he walked out to the boat and stayed on it the rest of the night to make sure that it didn't float away or sink. He wouldn't have concerned himself about the personal discomfort or risk. That was the sort of bloke he was.

Notes on the text

This book is primarily a memoir of my own experiences and recollections. In writing it, I was greatly assisted by the many people who appear in the narrative who made time to share their perspectives with me. It would also have been impossible to complete the project without consulting the excellent research, writing and photography dedicated to the subject of Broome and its pearling industry. Particular acknowledgement should be made of the following works: the helpful interviews which are part of the National Library of Australia's Broome oral history project (specifically, interviews with Kimberley Male, Pearl Hamaguchi, Richard Baillieu and Don McKenzie); Susan Sickert's excellent history *Beyond the Lattice: Broome's early years* (Fremantle Arts Centre Press, 2003), Donald Stuart and Roger Garwood's unforgettable *Broome: Landscapes and People* (Fremantle Arts Centre Press, 1983); *The Story of the Chinese in Broome* by Sarah Yu and Carol Tang Wei (published by the authors); Arthur C.V. Bligh's *The Golden Quest* (Publicity Press, 1955); Norman Bartlett's

The Pearl Seekers (Melrose, 1954); Peta Stephenson's *The Outsiders Within: Telling Australia's Indigenous–Asian Story* (UNSW Press, 2005); Karen Whitney's article, 'Dually disadvantaged: the impact of Anglo-European law on indigenous Australian Women', 4 James Cook U. L. Rev. 13 1997; Leonard Janiszewski and Effy Alexakis's article, 'White gold, deep blue: Greeks in the Australian pearling industry, 1880s–2007', published in *Greek Research in Australia: Proceedings of the Biennial International Conference of Greek Studies* (Flinders University, 2007); and Robert M. Wong's article, 'Pearl diving from Broome', published in a special supplement to SPUMS Journal, vol. 26, no. 1, 1 March 1996.

Acknowledgements

This book – almost seven years in gestation – would not have been possible without the help of many friends from Broome who shared the 1978–83 interval with me. They include Amy and Carol Tang Wei, Eunice Yu, Valerie Albert, Val Grechen, Nana King, Ramah Binti Buyong, Karen Smith, Carol Sharp, and the pearling mob, Richard Baillieu, (thanks for accommodation mate!), Norm House, Dave Harris, Shane Ford, Ross Barker, Penny and Steve Arrow, 'Agent Orange' brothers, Wayne and Larry House, Steve Zimmerle, ex-Roey bouncer, Carl Sputori, Mark Walsh, David Dureau, Steve Oats, Al Burton, Mick Bray, Kim Harvey, Dave Appleby and Lal, who all gave their time to trawl up long-dormant mental archives. Special thanks also to John Kelly, Nick Paspaley, Kim Male, Chris Cleveland, Dennis Carmody and Peter Vann in helping with details about significant corporate developments in the pearling industry. Don Greenlees for suggestions on the draft and a super big thanks to Syb Nolan who 'got it', Pan Mac's Tom Gilliatt for his vast reservoir of patience and Joel Naoum for LPL's splendid final fit-out. And finally gone but not forgotten, Bruce 'Big Bag' Barker, Graeme Hutton and Mannie Manolas.